At Issue

| Teen Suicide

Other Books in the At Issue Series:

At Issue

I Teen Suicide

Christine Watkins, Book Editor

GREENHAVEN PRESS
A part of Gale, Cengage Learning

GALE
CENGAGE Learning·

Detroit • New York • San Francisco • New Haven, Conn • Waterville, Maine • London

Elizabeth Des Chenes, *Director, Content Strategy*
Cynthia Sanner, *Publisher*
Douglas Dentino, *Manager, New Product*

For more information, contact:
Greenhaven Press
27500 Drake Rd.
Farmington Hills, MI 48331-3535
Or you can visit our Internet site at gale.cengage.com

For product information and technology assistance, contact us at

Gale Customer Support, 1-800-877-4253
For permission to use material from this text or product, submit all requests online at www.cengage.com/permissions

Further permissions questions can be emailed to permissionrequest@cengage.com

Articles in Greenhaven Press anthologies are often edited for length to meet page requirements. In addition, original titles of these works are changed to clearly present the main thesis and to explicitly indicate the author's opinion. Every effort is made to ensure that Greenhaven Press accurately reflects the original intent of the authors. Every effort has been made to trace the owners of copyrighted material.

Cover image © Images.com/Corbis.

LIBRARY OF CONGRESS CATALOGING-IN-PUBLICATION DATA

Teen suicide / Christine Watkins, book editor.
    p. cm. -- (At issue)
  Includes bibliographical references and index.
  ISBN 978-0-7377-6209-9 (hardcover) -- ISBN 978-0-7377-6210-5 (pbk.)
  1. Teenagers--Suicidal behavior--United States. 2. Teenagers--Mental health--United States. 3. Depression in adolescence--United States. 4. Adolescent psychology--United States. I. Watkins, Christine, 1951-
  HV6546.T422 2014
  362.280835'0973--dc23

                                        2013029612

Contents

Introduction

According to the American Psychiatric Association, suicide is the third leading cause of death for young people between eleven and eighteen years of age (behind accidents and homicide), and the suicide rate is highest for those who suffer from depression, substance abuse, or other mental disorders. Furthermore, the American College of Obstetricians and Gynecologists estimates that one in eight teenagers suffers from depression. Bill Brown, director of the 2007 film *The Hidden Epidemic*, describes depression as "an incredibly painful condition, and since it's human nature to seek pleasure and avoid pain . . . in the logic of depression the only remedy is to stop the pain, and that makes suicide a very desirable option." Adolescent depression often manifests as problems with memory, difficulty in concentrating and learning, mood swings, and persistent anxiety, all of which lead to withdrawal from family and friends. But what many people do not realize, and parents, physicians, coaches, and others are only recently becoming aware of, is that the symptoms of depression are the same symptoms of post concussion syndrome, or PCS. And just as depression can lead to suicide, so can PCS.

What is post concussion syndrome? A concussion is a jarring injury to the brain usually caused by a blow to the head or from another injury that shakes the brain inside the skull. According to the Slocum Center for Orthopedics and Sports Medicine in Eugene, Oregon, only about 5 to 10 percent of people are knocked unconscious with a concussion. Most are confused, dazed, or complain of a headache. Jonah Lehrer describes in his 2012 Grantland.com article, "The Fragile Teenage Brain," the effects of a concussion on the brain:

> "In the milliseconds after a concussion, there is a sudden release of neurotransmitters as billions of brain cells turn themselves on at the exact same time. This frenzy of activity

leads to a surge of electricity, an unleashing of the charged ions contained within neurons. It's as if the brain is pouring out its power. The worst part of the concussion, however, is what happens next, as all those cells frantically work to regain their equilibrium. . . . While the brain is restoring itself, people suffer from a long list of side effects, which are intended to keep them from thinking too hard. Bright lights are painful; memory is fragile and full of holes; focus is impossible. Because neurons are still starved for energy, even a minor 'secondary impact' can unleash a devastating molecular cascade. All of a sudden, brain cells that seemed to be regaining their balance begin committing suicide. The end result is a massive loss of neurons. . . . Teenagers are especially susceptible to these mass cellular suicides. This is largely because their brains are still developing, which means that even a slight loss of cells can alter the trajectory of brain growth."

Basically post concussion syndrome occurs when one or more symptoms—such as headache, sleepiness, confusion, blurred vision, balance problems, or vomiting—persist beyond ten to fourteen days following a concussion.

Hundreds of thousands of adolescents receive concussions every year, many of which are not diagnosed properly. According to Dr. Robert Cantu, clinical professor of neurosurgery and codirector of Boston University's Center for the Study of Traumatic Encephalopathy, "What's happening in this country is an epidemic of concussions, number one, and the realization that many of these individuals are going to go on to post-concussion syndrome, which can alter their ability to function at a high level for the rest of their lives." And it is this altered state of mental confusion and anxiety that can lead to severe depression, which can then result in suicide. Take, for example, the case of seventeen-year-old Austin Trenum, who played linebacker and fullback on his high school football team. Austin had mentioned to friends about getting "football headaches" after every game and had suffered at least one concussion the previous season. On this particular Friday night in 2010, Austin received another concussion while tackling the opposing team's quarterback. Two days later on Sunday afternoon, he hanged himself in his room at home. Doctors later discovered structural damage to the portion of Austin's brain that affects judgment and impulse control, and Austin's parents are certain the concussion caused his suicide.

And consider fifteen-year-old Allison Kasacavage of Chester Springs, Pennsylvania. She is able to attend only four hours of school a day because of intense headaches, dizziness, nausea, and vision problems resulting from at least five concussions received while playing soccer. Allison told Kate Snow in a 2012 interview for NBC News's *Rock Center with Brian Williams*, "It's almost like I need a sign on my back saying, 'My head is broken.'" In fact, the number of concussions related to girls' soccer is second only to the number reported by young football players. Snow reported, "along with their physical ailments, several of the girls NBC News spoke to have struggled with depression since leaving soccer. Some have taken antidepressants. One teen soccer player, who is returning to the sport after suffering a concussion, said that she felt so terrible at one point that she even thought about suicide."

Not all concussions cause longterm problems, but many do; therefore, all concussions should be taken seriously. Sports injury experts advise that coaches, parents, and players themselves become better educated about the symptoms and effects of this type of traumatic brain injury. They also believe that pediatricians should be trained in concussion management, including the importance of baseline concussion testing. Furthermore, because depression and withdrawal can be indicative of PCS, constant vigilance by parents and even a therapist is vital to monitor symptoms and suggest possible treatment. The authors of the viewpoints in *At Issue: Teen Suicide* discuss other aspects concerning the risks and possible solutions surrounding the problem of teen suicide.

1

Teen Suicide Is a Major Health Problem

Michiko Otsuki, Tia Kim, and Paul Peterson

Michiko Otsuki is an assistant professor in the psychology department at the University of South Florida St. Petersburg College of Arts and Sciences. Tia Kim is an assistant professor in the department of human development and family studies at Pennsylvania State University, Brandywine. Paul Peterson is an active psychotherapist with a practice in Utah.

Thousands of America's youth commit suicide every year, with American Indian/Alaska Native youth having the highest rate across all age groups. Immigrant youth as well as gay, lesbian, and bisexual youth also have an elevated risk for suicide because of the stress associated with fitting in with their peers. Other common risk factors to look out for in teens are major depression, prior attempts at suicide, and a stressful home life. School screening programs to identify high-risk students have proven to be effective tools in suicide prevention efforts; restricting access to means of committing suicide—such as removing firearms from the home—also shows promising results in reducing teen suicide.

Youth suicide is a major public health problem in the United States today. Each year in the U.S., thousands of teenagers commit suicide. Suicide is the third leading cause of death for 15–24 year olds, and the fifth leading cause of death for 5–14 year olds. The reduction of adolescent suicide is one of the major objectives of the Healthy People 2010 Initiative [of the US Department of Health and Human Services].

Suicide is less common during childhood and the early teen years. In 2006, the rate was .5 suicides per 100,000 children aged 10–14. Suicide mortality increases considerably in the late teens and continues into the early twenties for both males and females. Although females are more likely than males to attempt suicide, males are roughly five times as likely to succeed in their suicide attempts.

American Indian/Alaska Native youth have the highest prevalence of suicide across all age groups. In this group males have the higher prevalence. European-American youth have the next highest prevalence. Their prevalence is higher than that of African-American, Latino, and Asian-American/Pacific Islander youth. Although research suggests that Native American and Latino youth have the highest suicide-related fatalities, Latino female youth are more likely to attempt suicide than all other groups of youth.

One quarter to one-third of youth suicide victims make suicide attempts prior to their completed suicide.

Firearm death remains the most prevalent method of suicide, regardless of age, gender, and ethnicity. It accounts for 46% of suicide deaths among youths. The second and third most prevalent methods of youth suicide are hanging and poisoning, respectively. The gender difference in the rates of completed suicide is largely explained by the gender differences in suicide methods. Females are more likely to poison themselves whereas males are more likely to shoot themselves. Firearms are more lethal than poison.

Behavioral Warning Signs of Suicide Risk

For every completed suicide, an estimated 100 to 200 suicide attempts are made. Attempted suicides are a risk factor for successful suicide.

Suicidal behaviors are complex and have multiple risk factors.

The majority of youth who have completed suicide had significant psychiatric problems, including depressive disorders and substance abuse disorders. Major depression has been the most prevalent condition. The intensity of a person's suicidal intent is associated with a history of depression and anxiety and current stress from a mental disorder. Although many mental disorders increase the odds of suicide ideation, disorders characterized by anxiety and poor impulse control increase the odds of actual suicide attempts. Female youth suicides have a higher prevalence of an affective disorder than male youth suicides. Substance abuse is also a significant risk factor, especially for older adolescent male victims and when co-occurring with an affective disorder.

One quarter to one-third of youth suicide victims make suicide attempts prior to their completed suicide. Anxiety lowers the likelihood of one-time suicide attempts but increases the likelihood of repeated suicide attempts. With each successive attempt, the risk of completed suicide increases—for male adolescents the risk is thirty times higher, whereas for female adolescents the risk is three times higher.

Given that death by firearms is the most common method of youth suicide, it is not surprising that the accessibility and availability of firearms, particularly loaded guns, in the home increase the risk of youth suicide. The home is the most common location for firearm suicides by youth.

Maladaptive coping skills and poor interpersonal skills limit adolescents' ability to problem solve, thereby increasing the likelihood that suicide will be considered the only solution. Early youth substance use also increases the risk of suicidal behaviors.

Adolescents who attempt or complete suicide experience multiple negative life events. The events may have occurred in childhood, such as physical and/or sexual abuse, neglect, separation and previous suicide attempts. These stressors often overwhelm the coping skills of the adolescent because of his/her inexperience with such life situations. Other life events are also associated with suicide risk: interpersonal losses (e.g., breaking up with a boyfriend/girlfriend), legal or disciplinary problems (e.g., getting into trouble at schools or with a law enforcement agency), and victimization by peers. The experience of a disproportionate number of stressful life events may compound problem-solving difficulties present in the youth.

Untreated depression and substance abuse disorders are major causes of adolescent suicide.

Exposure to suicide increases the likelihood of suicide. For example, the number of suicides goes up following the appearance of suicide stories in the mass media, including newspaper articles, television news reports, and fictional and nonfictional dramatization. The influence of suicide stories is greatest among adolescents and is diminished greatly after the age of 24.

Several family factors are associated with an increased likelihood of youth suicide: poor family relationships, a family history of suicidal behaviors, obligation to the family, and parental psychopathology namely, depression and substance abuse. Some research also points to genetic factors to explain the link between parental characteristics and youth suicide.

Predisposing Characteristics for Potential Suicide Risk

Little is known about the association between socioeconomic status and youth suicide. Low socioeconomic status may increase suicide risk if it is associated with barriers to mental health treatment, given that untreated depression and substance abuse disorders are major causes of adolescent suicide.

Among Latinos, being born in the United States is associated with a higher risk of suicide than being foreign-born Latino youths. However, immigrant youths often experience stress associated with acculturation. The elevated stress level among immigrants has been offered as an explanation of the higher risk of non-lethal suicidal attempts among Latino youth. Studies have shown that both the association between psychopathology and suicidal behavior and the association between drug use and suicidal behavior are dependent on the degree of acculturative stress.

Relative to their heterosexual peers, gay, lesbian, and bisexual (GLB) youth are at an elevated risk for suicide. Discrimination causes depression among GLB adolescents, elevating the risk of suicidal ideation and self harm. In addition, GLB youth are at high risk for associated maladaptive risk behaviors, including fighting, victimization, and drug use.

Abnormalities in the serotonergic system are associated with suicidal behaviors. For example, low levels of serotonin among suicide attempters were predictive of future completion of suicide. However, exposure to SSRIs [selective serotonin reuptake inhibitor class of compounds used as antidepressants] has also been shown to increase risk of completed or attempted suicide among adolescents. Other data suggest that an abnormal neurotrophin system contributes to a tendency toward suicide.

Developing Strategies to Prevent Teen Suicide

The application of knowledge of suicide etiology to the design and evaluation of prevention strategies has just begun. According to the CDC [Centers for Disease Control and Prevention], the goals of youth suicide prevention strategies are twofold: risk factor reduction and case finding.

Additional prevention efforts to reduce youth suicide need to be designed, implemented, and evaluated.

Risk reduction strategies include suicide prevention for youth and the community and involve: (a) promoting overall mental health among school-aged youth by reducing early risk factors for depression, substance abuse, and aggression, and building resiliency (e.g., self-esteem and stress management); (b) providing crisis counseling; and (c) restricting access to lethal means, especially, handguns. Promotion of mental health among school-aged youth is typically achieved by general suicide education and peer support programs. General suicide education is designed to develop healthy peer relationship and social skills among high-risk adolescents. It provides youth with information about suicide, including its warning signs, and how to seek professional help for themselves or others. Crisis counseling through crisis centers and hotlines involves trained volunteers and paid staff providing counseling via phone or drop-by services for suicidal youth. Postventions are interventions after an incidence of both successful and unsuccessful suicide attempts. These programs aim at preventing suicide contagion and helping youth and family cope effectively with an interpersonal loss following a suicide. Interventions restricting access to lethal means are designed to reduce a person's access to lethal means of completing suicide, such as through disposal of medications and removal and/or lock up of firearms from the home of a suicidal adolescent.

Case finding strategies may be active or passive and aim at detecting suicidal youth by referral to mental health care. A sample active strategy is general screening programs or a targeted screening program after a suicide. In screening programs, self-reports and individual interviews are administered to identify depression, alcohol or substance abuse problems, recent suicidal ideation, and past suicide attempts. Further detailed assessment and treatment are provided where necessary. Sample passive strategies include gatekeeper training for schoolteachers and community adults, general suicide education in schools, and crisis counseling. Gatekeeper training involves educating and training adults in contact with suicidal youth such as school staff (e.g., teachers, counselors, and coaches) and community members (e.g., physicians, clergy, and police) to identify and refer children and adolescents at risk for suicide. General education efforts aim to reduce the stigma associated with accessing mental health care and to increase self-referral and/or referrals by persons who recognize suicidality in someone they know.

Current prevention efforts are in need of evaluation. Available evidence shows that interventions restricting access to lethal suicide means are among the most promising efforts. Studies on the effectiveness of general suicide education in schools are equivocal, with some research showing iatrogenic [medical treatment] effects of intervention. Screening programs have been found to be effective in identifying high-risk students. Crisis centers and hotlines are largely unevaluated.

Clearly, additional prevention efforts to reduce youth suicide need to be designed, implemented, and evaluated. Due to the enormous effort and financial cost involved in launching and maintaining programs, the efficacy and safety of the programs should be guaranteed before they are promoted. The CDC's (1994) recommendations include ensuring that prevention programs are matched with access to mental health resources in the community, incorporate several prevention strategies, and incorporate rigorous scientific planning, process, and outcome evaluations.

2

Suicide Myths Hamper Preventive Efforts

Tennessee Suicide Prevention Network

The Tennessee Suicide Prevention Network (TSPN) is a grass-roots association that includes mental health professionals, physicians, social workers, and law enforcement personnel, as well as survivors of suicide attempts. TSPN works to eliminate the stigma of suicide and educate communities statewide with the ultimate goal of reducing suicide rates.

The subject of suicide can be unpleasant to think about, but the fact remains that suicide is the third leading cause of death for people aged ten to thirty-four. And depression, which sometimes leads to suicide, is widespread among teenagers and can even affect children as young as eight or nine years old. Knowledge about suicide is a powerful tool in suicide prevention. For example, many people believe that discussing suicide with a suicidal person will make the problem worse when, in fact, it often will make things better.

In the United States alone, someone dies by suicide once every 16 minutes. Suicide is the third leading cause of death for youth and young adults between the ages of 10 and 34. But because suicide has been considered such a "taboo" subject to think or to talk about, there are a lot of misconceptions about which individuals may be at risk, about when, how and why people might consider killing themselves, and about how best to help yourself or someone else who's contemplating suicide.

This misinformation—or the lack of information altogether—often means that desperate people can't get the help they need in times of crisis. Being well-informed about depression and suicide can help you save your own life or the life of someone you know or love!

Myths and Facts About Youth Suicide

Myth: "Only adults can get truly depressed."

Fact: Kids as young as 8 or 9 can get severely depressed. Depression is epidemic among teens today.

Myth: "Depression is a weakness."

Fact: Depression is a serious but treatable illness that has nothing to do with moral strength or weakness.

Myth: "Depression is mostly a white, middle class problem."

Fact: Depression is an "equal opportunity illness" that can affect anyone, regardless of race or socioeconomic level. Depression and suicide rates among young African-American males and Hispanic teenage girls in particular have dramatically increased in the past 20 years.

People who are thinking about suicide usually find some way of communicating their pain to others.

Myth: "Only depressed kids attempt suicide."

Fact: Kids don't have to be clinically depressed to have suicidal feelings or to attempt suicide. Even feeling extremely "bummed out" for a relatively short period of time can lead to impulsive suicide attempts. Nevertheless, a person who is clinically depressed for longer periods of time is at higher risk for attempting suicide.

Myth: "People who are depressed always feel sad."

19

Fact: Other symptoms of depression can be irritability, lack of energy, change in appetite, substance abuse, restlessness, racing thoughts, reckless behavior, too much or too little sleep, or otherwise unexplained physical ailments.

Myth: "People who talk about suicide don't kill themselves."

Fact: People who are thinking about suicide usually find some way of communicating their pain to others—often by speaking indirectly about their intentions. Most suicidal people will admit to their feelings if questioned directly.

Myth: "There's really nothing you can do to help someone who's truly suicidal."

Fact: Most people who are suicidal don't really want their lives to end—they just want the pain to end. The understanding, support, and hope that you offer can be their most important lifeline.

Myth: "Discussing suicide may cause someone to consider it or make things worse."

Fact: Asking someone if they're suicidal will never give them an idea that they haven't thought about already. Most suicidal people are truthful and relieved when questioned about their feelings and intentions. Doing so can be the first step in helping them to choose to live.

Never, ever keep you or someone else's suicidal thoughts and feelings a secret.

Myth: "Telling someone to cheer up usually helps."

Fact: Trying to cheer someone up might make them feel even more misunderstood and ashamed of their thoughts and feelings. It's important to listen well and take them seriously.

Myth: "It's best to keep someone's suicidal feelings a secret."

Fact: Never, ever keep your or someone else's suicidal thoughts and feelings a secret—even if you're asked to do so. Friends never keep deadly secrets!

Myth: "If someone promised to seek help, your job is done."

Fact: You need to make sure that any suicidal person stays safe until you can help them connect with a responsible adult.

Myths and Facts About Adult Suicide

Myth: "People who complete suicide always leave notes."

Fact: Most people don't leave notes.

Myth: "People who die from suicide don't warn others."

Over 70% who do threaten to carry out a suicide either make an attempt or complete the act.

Fact: Out of 10 people who kill themselves, eight have given definite clues to their intentions. They leave numerous clues and warnings to others, although some of their clues may be nonverbal or difficult to detect.

Myth: "People who talk about suicide are only trying to get attention. They won't really do it."

Fact: WRONG! Few people commit suicide without first letting someone else know how they feel. Those who are considering suicide give clues and warnings as a cry for help. In fact, most seek out someone to rescue them. Over 70% who do threaten to carry out a suicide either make an attempt or complete the act.

Myth: "Once someone has already decided on suicide, nothing is going to stop them. Suicidal people clearly want to die."

Fact: Most of the time, a suicidal person is ambivalent about the decision; they are torn between wanting to die and wanting to live. Most suicidal individuals don't want death; they just want the pain to stop. Some people, seeing evidence

21

of two conflicting feelings in the individual may interpret the action as insincerity: "He really doesn't want to do it; I don't think he is serious." People's ability to help is hindered if they don't understand the common suicidal characteristic of ambivalence.

Myth: "Once the emotional state improves, the risk of suicide is over."

Fact: The highest rates of suicide occur within about three months of an apparent improvement in a severely depressed state. Therefore, an improvement in emotional state doesn't mean a lessened risk.

Myth: "After a person has attempted suicide, it is unlikely he/she will try again."

Fact: People who have attempted suicide are very likely to try again. 80% of the people who die from suicide have made at least one previous attempt.

Myth: "You shouldn't mention suicide to someone who's showing signs of severe depression. It will plant the idea in their minds, and they will act on it."

Fact: Many depressed people have already considered suicide as an option. Discussing it openly helps the suicidal person sort through the problems and generally provides a sense of relief and understanding. It is one of the most helpful things you can do.

Myth: "If someone survives a suicide attempt, they weren't serious about ending their life."

Fact: The attempt in and of itself is the most important factor, not the effectiveness of the method.

3

Bullying Increases the Risk of Teen Suicide

Michael Ollove

Michael Ollove, previously an editor and reporter at The Baltimore Sun *newspaper, is now senior editor for the journal* Health Affairs.

Adolescents, teenagers, parents, and educators—indeed all Americans—need to confront the growing problem of bullying and its consequences. One out of every three students between twelve and eighteen years of age claim to have been bullied. And in several cases teens reportedly committed suicide to escape the intense and unrelenting bullying they endured, giving rise to the term "bullycide." Bullying should no longer be trivialized as "kids just being kids" or accepted because "kids need to learn to stand up for themselves." Bullying is an assault, and until people recognize it as such and take steps to prevent it, teens will continue to commit bullycide.

If you could judge a school by its cover, northwest Georgia's Murray County High would be a most genial place to be educated.

A small forest of blossoming Bradford pear trees ushers students toward a cheery, single-story building of pale formstone and distinctive archways underneath a nearly fluorescent, pepper-green roof. In a grassy median in front, a jolly, metallic statue of the school's mascot, an Indian warrior, rises up in greeting.

If these features were meant to suggest a warm educational embrace, it is fair to say that they were lost on 17-year-old Tyler Lee Long. Whatever else he may have thought of Murray High, it was certainly not as a benign place. In his mind, the school might as well have been encased in barbed wire with gargoyles leering down at him from the facade. For Tyler, who suffered from Asperger's Disorder [an autism spectrum disorder characterized by social and communication difficulties], Murray High was little more than a torture chamber, where—his parents say and students confirm—he felt himself subjected to unending humiliation at the hands of some of his fellow students under the indifferent watch of teachers and administrators.

"Bullycides" have drawn attention to the overall problem of bullying and the responsibility of schools to put a stop to it.

Drawing Attention to the Growing Problem of "Bullycide"

Last October [2009], two months into his junior year, Tyler could bear it no longer. He had brighter dreams of his future—he was two weeks from earning his black belt in karate, and he envisioned attending the University of Texas and one day designing the sort of computer games he loved playing. But none of that was enough to keep him going back to Murray High.

So on Oct. 17, after his family had gone to bed, he changed out of his pajamas into his favorite black T-shirt and jeans, strapped one of his belts around his neck, opened the louvered doors of his bedroom closet, and hanged himself from a shelf.

Tyler's suicide note does not specifically mention bullying as the reason for his action, but his parents, Tina and David Long, have no doubt why he took his life. "Tyler didn't want to be bullied any longer," Mrs. Long says evenly in the family's Colonial house about 35 miles southeast of Chattanooga [Tennessee], "and that is the bottom line."

In other words, say the Longs, Tyler committed "bullycide," a term increasingly finding its way into the educational lexicon as a result of several teen suicides that were attributed at least in part to bullying. Most recently—in March [2010]—the term pierced national consciousness when a Massachusetts district attorney indicted nine students on criminal charges arising from the suicide of a 15-year-old Irish immigrant named Phoebe Prince who also hanged herself after experiencing persistent bullying.

Also in March, the Longs filed a lawsuit in federal court against the Murray County School District and Murray High School principal Gail Linder for allegedly failing to protect Tyler despite many entreaties from his parents.

There are no reliable statistics that break out the number of teen suicides attributable to bullying. In most cases it may not be possible to definitively attribute a teen's suicide to a particular cause, be it bullying, a broken heart, a bad test score, or simply chronic depression. Nevertheless, the cases of so-called "bullycides" have drawn attention to the overall problem of bullying and the responsibility of schools to put a stop to it.

Certainly, the Longs believe the Murray County Schools had a responsibility to their son, and they intend the lawsuit to emphatically make that clear.

"They need to be held accountable for Tyler's death," says Mr. Long. "The reason we're speaking [up] is to protect these kids and make schools aware [that] when the parents or student tell you something, you don't turn the other cheek."

Through Atlanta attorney Martha Pearson, the Murray County School District and Ms. Linder deny the allegations: "There was no information that the district had surrounding this child's suicide that he had been subjected to repeated bullying. The school simply did not have that kind of information, and anytime Tyler had any problem associated with his disability the school was responsive."

In the wake of other deaths attributed to bullying, school districts similarly say the bullying occurred without the knowledge of school officials. But increasingly parents and educators are saying that isn't good enough, that schools cannot take a see no evil approach.

"Schools will say, 'Oh it's just kids being kids, it's a rite of passage.' But it's an assault. We don't allow people to abuse the elderly or pets and we're not going to allow abuse when it's peer on peer, either," says Monica Thomas, who started an anti-bulling website when she felt she got no help from her son's Pennsylvania high school with her complaints that he was being bullied.

Repudiating Established Myths Regarding Bullies

As tragic as the suicides of Tyler and Phoebe are, their deaths and other bullycides draw more attention to the subject of bullying and its consequences, which educators hope will lead to more prevention programs.

One-third of American kids face bullying.

"This is going to give a whole new complexion to bullying and prevention here in the United States," says Marlene Snyder, director of development for an antibullying program used in many American schools. "The message that needs to get out is you need to pay attention to what the kids are doing and there are programs out there that can help."

As any American teenager could tell you, bullying isn't rare. The National Center for Educational Statistics, in 2009, said nearly 1 in 3 students between the ages of 12 and 18 reported being bullied in school. Eight years earlier, only 14 percent of that population said they had experienced bullying.

The good news, experts agree, is that almost certainly some of that increase can be attributed to better reporting as a result of bullying prevention programs that encourage victims to confide in adults when bullied. The sobering news, though, is that one-third of American kids face bullying.

Increasingly, educators recognize that bullying has a detrimental effect on learning. "In schools where this behavior is allowed to run rampant, it damages the whole school," says Ms. Snyder. "It can ruin a school environment.". . .

Experts in the field say that addressing bullying means disabusing traditional notions on the subject. One of the most persistent myths is that bullying is an expected aspect of growing up, a normal rite of passage that is healthy to face and to face down. Not only is that thinking wrong, says Snyder, it is dangerous.

Bullying, she says, isn't a conflict between equals. It's intentional, persistent, humiliating mistreatment between peers, dished out by those more powerful than their targets by virtue of size, age, numbers, status, money, race, or other characteristics. It's not a debate, argument, or difference of opinion. It's an act of aggression intended to do harm.

"Kids who have been bullied have different facial expressions," says Snyder. "They look humiliated, devastated. That's not the result of conflict between people of equal power who merely have a disagreement."

Victims, by virtue of their age, aren't often equipped to let the impact of these incidents roll off their shoulders, she says.

"Students don't have the life experience to know that this is going to change, that it won't always be like this."

Studies show that bullying often causes depression, further isolation, absenteeism, an aversion to risk-taking, and poor academic performance. Most of the time, the victim can't handle the problem without help. Another major myth—portrayed endlessly on film and television—is that standing up to the bully is an effective strategy, say experts.

Cyberbullying is rising, particularly among girls.

For one thing, the bully usually has the advantage in size or numbers. For another, contrary to popular wisdom, bullies are usually not dummies suffering from low self-esteem. Studies show that bullies tend to have above-average intelligence and an excess of self-regard. They view themselves as entitled, an inadvertent outgrowth, says Stan Davis, an antibullying consultant in Maine, of a culture that stresses every person's specialness and uniqueness while perhaps giving short shrift to empathy. "We need to emphasize similarity," Mr. Davis says, "not uniqueness."

Expecting the targets of bullying to deal with it on their own—either by fighting back, ignoring it, or trying to appeal to the bully's sympathy, are not effective strategies and is unfair to the victim, says Davis. "You're basically telling the kid, 'Not only are you being mistreated, but it's your fault.'". . .

Educating Kids About the Harm from Cyberbullying

Surveys show that incidents of physical bullying are lessening across the country. At the same time, cyberbullying is rising, particularly among girls. It's easy to see why. Experts say technology removes inhibitions and cushions the perpetrator from the consequences of his or her actions.

"People whose empathy would deter them if they could see the pain in the other person's face, feel emboldened to do it when they cannot see that person's face," says Davis. "And in an instant, they can spread that damage across their entire electronic contact list."

Often cyberbullying is beyond the reach of schools, but, says Patti Agatston, an antibullying counselor in Cobb County, Ga., and creator of cyberbullying curriculum, school programs should make clear that it is still bullying even when it isn't face to face: "We have to educate kids [so they know that] the way we treat each other on the Internet can be bullying." In some ways, she says, virtual bullying can be even worse. With face-to-face bullying, you can at least leave it behind when you go home. Not so with Internet bullying. Plus, the taunting from a bully on the Web can be witnessed by so many more than in a physical setting.

Like face-to-face bullying, cyberbullying often targets those who are different. Smaller kids. Minorities. Heavy-set kids. Kids with disabilities.

"My son had a little bit of a speech problem," says Mrs. Thomas, whose son Joey was harassed all through high school. Joey's words would come out slurry, almost as though he were drunk. He was also barely 5'3", had a bad case of acne, and was, by his own description, a bit of a goofball. All of that made fodder for taunting and worse—pushing and punching. "I had a lot of anger, hate, and depression," says Joey, now 20. "It made me think, 'Why am I even here?'" He thought about suicide.

Personifying the Impact of Bullying

Tyler Lee Long also was different. As a young child he lagged far behind others in starting to talk and walk. In elementary school, he didn't make eye contact, hated to be touched, and was unable to connect with other kids. And he insisted on certain set routines. "At 3, he wouldn't eat anything but Burger

King chicken and limeade Gatorade," says Mr. Long, a manager with a carpet manufacturer. "It got so every day we'd pull up to the window and they'd say, 'The usual, Mr. Long?'"

Mrs. Long hoped that the bullying would lessen in high school, that the kids would mature out of it. . . . [But the] bullying merely intensified.

In sixth grade, Tyler was diagnosed with Asperger's Disorder, a milder form of autism. His cognitive abilities were normal—he took honors and AP [advanced placement] classes in high school—but social interaction seemed beyond him. At the time of his death, his mother, Tina, a nurse, says he had no real friends, only virtual ones encountered on the Web. He enjoyed fishing, golf, and karate. "Karate is very structured, very literal, very ritualized," says Mrs. Long. "It fit in with the way he thought." And unlike at school, she says, the karate teacher wouldn't stand for kids picking on one another.

The bullying started at the end of fifth grade, Mrs. Long says, when a kid started taunting Tyler and pushing him around. From then on, it was almost ceaseless name-calling and shoving, she says.

Mrs. Long complained to teachers, administrators, and counselors in the middle school and high school. Some years they weren't responsive, she says, some years they were. In the seventh grade, a teacher was assigned to walk Tyler to the bus and through the halls, and to sit with him in the cafeteria.

Mrs. Long hoped that the bullying would lessen in high school, that the kids would mature out of it. What she found, she says, was that "they were sneakier."

The bullying merely intensified. Tyler's brother Troy and sister Teryn—twins two years younger than Tyler—often witnessed the episodes on the bus they shared. They tried to intervene. Sometimes it helped, but never for long. Neither, says their mother, did the complaints to school officials.

"The school would respond to Tyler and to us, 'Oh, they didn't mean it,'" says Mrs. Long.

"'Boys will be boys,'" Mr. Long adds.

Tyler was less inclined to tell his parents [about the bullying]. He was embarrassed, and he also no longer wanted his parents to try to intervene.

"Or, 'He just took it the wrong way,'" says Mrs. Long. If there was an antibullying program, she notes, "I was not aware of it."

At the beginning of his sophomore year, according to the Longs' lawsuit, Tyler was pushed down a flight of stairs. The suit claims the school took no action to punish the perpetrators or protect Tyler.

The bullying continued, but Tyler was less inclined to tell his parents. He was embarrassed, and he also no longer wanted his parents to try to intervene. "The more you call up there," he told his mother, "the worse it is for me."

But the bullying continued anyway. On. Oct. 15, last year [2009], according to the lawsuit, a student taunted Tyler and chased him around a music class while the teacher was out of the room. The next day, the abuse resumed, and later, a student pushed Tyler's head into a locker. Another student spat in his food and told him to "hang himself." The harassment continued on the bus home that night, even after Tyler moved to the back to avoid his tormenters.

In its answer to the Longs' lawsuit, the Murray County School District denies that Tyler had been "constantly bullied" and takes issue with virtually all of the specific allegations in the complaint. "[N]o 'brutal and systemic pattern of bullying' of Tyler Long occurred," the school system says, reprising language from the Longs' lawsuit.

A police investigation also did not substantiate any of the specific allegations of bullying in Tyler's last days, and the Chatsworth Police Department chose not to file criminal charges.

The conflict sets up the probability that numerous teenagers will find themselves on the witness stand if the case reaches trial. Winston Briggs, the Longs' Atlanta [Georgia] attorney, insists that their testimony will resonate in schools across the country: "There's no question that this case and this issue has national implications and could reach a national audience and should reach a national audience so this type of tragedy is averted by some other family."

If Tyler had been bullied in mid-October, his parents say they didn't know it at the time. By then Tyler no longer wanted them to know what was happening. Everyone went to bed as usual that Friday night, Oct. 16. Early the next morning, the cat woke up Mr. Long to be let out. As he always did, he poked his head into the kids' rooms to make sure they were all right. Tyler wasn't in bed. Alarmed, he stepped into the room and saw his son slumped in the closet. He began screaming.

All of Tyler's furniture has been moved out of the room, which is now an office. A large photograph of Tyler in his ROTC [Reserve Officers' Training Corps] uniform looks over his former bedroom.

The room and the house were a sanctuary for Tyler, the place he felt safe and knew he was accepted. As for not having any real friends, Mrs. Long says, it didn't seem to bother him. "He didn't mind being alone. It was OK with him."

But the bullying that he perceived was not. He couldn't bear it, and he couldn't stop it, so he chose what he thought was his only option, she says.

"This," says his mother, "was his way of having peace."

4

Bullying and Suicide: The Dangerous Mistake We Make

Katherine Bindley

Katherine Bindley writes about culture and style for The Huffington Post. *She has worked as a reporter for the* New York Times *and has written for the* Wall Street Journal.

A spate of teen suicides throughout the past several years has been blamed on bullying. On closer examination, however, the root cause of these suicides is usually much more complicated. Very often a history of unresolved emotional issues or underlying mental health illnesses, such as depression and anxiety, are present in these teens. The additional stress from being bullied can then be the final stimulus for turning to suicide as the only way out. If suicide prevention programs focus only on bullying, the programs will have limited, if any, success. A broad spectrum approach that includes awareness of and help for mental health issues will be much more effective in preventing teen suicide.

Tyler Clementi killed himself in 2010 after his roommate at Rutgers University filmed him kissing another man. Phoebe Prince, a 15-year-old girl who moved to the U.S. from Ireland, killed herself the same year after being bullied by high school classmates in Massachusetts. Fifteen-year-old Amanda

Cummings from Staten Island made headlines early this January [2012] when her family said that relentless bullying was to blame for her suicide.

Each of these tragedies mobilized a cultural army of anti-bullying advocates, celebrities, the media and policymakers who have said—or at least strongly implied—that bullying can lead to suicide.

But mental health professionals and those who work in suicide prevention say bullying-related suicides that reach the spotlight are painted far too simplistically. Bullying and suicide can indeed be connected, though the relationship between the two is much more complicated than a tabloid headline might suggest. To imply clear-cut lines of cause and effect, many experts maintain, is misleading and potentially damaging as it ignores key underlying mental health issues, such as depression and anxiety.

"Bullying is so at the top of our consciousness that we're bending over backwards to get it into the story," said Ann Haas, a senior project specialist with the American Foundation for Suicide Prevention. "Years and years of research has taught us that the overwhelming number of people who die by suicide had a diagnosable mental disorder at the time of their death."

Bullying can offer an answer . . . : "It's almost easier to understand—someone was victimized, and then they killed themselves."

Haas argues that failing to look at the other contributing factors, from depression to family life to the ending of a relationship, is problematic and even perilous from a suicide prevention standpoint. "I am very concerned about the narrative that these stories collectively are writing, which is that suicide is a normal, understandable response to this terrible [bullying] behavior," said Haas. "In suicide prevention, we tend to favor the explanation that there are multiple causes."

Lidia Bernik, an associate project director with National Suicide Prevention Lifeline, said that people often seek a simple explanation when something as difficult to understand as suicide occurs. "I speak from personal experience," she said. "I lost my sister to suicide. You're left with, 'Why did this happen?'"

Bullying can offer an answer, she said: "It's almost easier to understand—someone was victimized, and then they killed themselves."

Nicole Cardarelli, 27, who works in state advocacy outreach for the American Foundation for Suicide Prevention, admits that for years after her brother Greg's suicide in 2004, she also blamed bullying. While in high school, Greg began what he thought was a relationship with a girl he met online in a Ford Thunderbird car club. It turned out that two of his friends were behind the fake account. After several months, the boys exposed the prank to Greg. Hours later, he killed himself. His family opted not to press charges but they couldn't help placing blame when Greg had named what the boys did in his suicide note as the reason he could no longer go on living.

"If you had asked me after Greg died what I wanted to have happen, I probably would have said I want to kill those boys," said Cardarelli. "It's so much harder to look at the person you loved so much and ask, what was going on inside him?"

At the time, Cardarelli didn't see the signs that Greg was troubled, she recalled. But in the subsequent years, she has thought about his behavior a few months before he died. He had lost interest in baseball and Boy Scouts—two activities he'd been involved with for years. He was sleeping more than usual, pulling away from his family and spending a lot of time on his computer. Cardarelli even remembers a conversation where her mother told her she thought there might be something really wrong with Greg.

"I believe that he was depressed," she said recently.

Just as that suicide may have been more complicated than Cardarelli initially thought, several high-profile cases have exhibited similar, deeper patterns upon further investigation.

Emily Bazelon's 2010 article for *Slate* exploring the suicide of Phoebe Prince, the teen from Ireland, serves as a powerful example of what can be learned when a suicide is examined more closely. There's no doubt that Prince endured cruel treatment from a group of classmates, but Bazelon reported that Prince had attempted suicide in the past, that she'd gone off antidepressants, and that she frequently cut herself. (In December, Bazelon followed up on the Prince case by reporting that Prince's family members had reached a settlement with the town of the South Hadley, Mass., for $225,000.)

Even though suicides often prove to involve multiple factors, most experts are still quick to add that bullying can aggravate depression and increase suicide risk.

The death of Staten Island teen Amanda Cummings, whose family primarily blamed bullying for her death, is proving to be less straight-forward as well. The NYPD has yet to find any evidence of bullying, and she was reportedly devastated over the end of a relationship with an older boy.

Last week, the *New Yorker* revisited the Clementi case at Rutgers from 2010 and offered a more nuanced view of the tragedy. News stories initially reported that Clementi was outed by his roommate, and that the video of him with another man was posted to the Internet, neither of which is true.

According to the *New Yorker*, Clementi came out to family members three days before he started at Rutgers—he told a friend his mother didn't respond well—and he attended a meeting of the school's Bisexual, Gay, and Lesbian Alliance. Documents found on Clementi's computer, the piece reported, were titled "sorry" and "Why is everything so painful." He had told a friend, "I would consider myself out if only there was someone for me to come out to." His roommate's actions were reprehensible, and they may have contributed to Clementi's death, but these new details suggest the possibility of a far more complex situation.

The prevalence of bullying has likely been overstated.

Even though suicides often prove to involve multiple factors, most experts are still quick to add that bullying can aggravate depression and increase suicide risk, and its seriousness shouldn't be minimized.

Clayton Cook, a professor of educational psychology at the University of Washington, argues that because mental health issues are often a common thread running through bullying and suicide, schools should not have a narrowly-focused solution.

"The idea is that if you adopt a broad spectrum approach to preventing mental health problems, that you're also going to reduce the bullying," said Cook. "If you look at the scientific literature, bullying prevention programs haven't shown to be effective. It's addressing the symptom and not the cause." Cook suggests teachers adopt a social emotional learning curriculum as they would a reading curriculum. "We'd teach kids how to exhibit care and concern for others, how to manage their emotions before they get the best of them," Cook explained.

The good news, according to Cook, is that the prevalence of bullying has likely been overstated. Catherine Bradshaw, deputy director of the Center for the Prevention of Youth Violence at Johns Hopkins, agrees. "We don't have data to show that bullying is an epidemic or that it's increasing," she said.

The Centers for Disease Control's bullying task force, of which Cook and Bradshaw are members, is working to establish a uniform definition of bullying for research purposes, but results may not be available until this summer. The task force is treating bullying as a public health concern and developing policy-based solutions.

As far as the prevalence of youth suicide goes, the most recent numbers from the CDC show that, among 15- to 19-year-olds, suicides fell marginally from 8.02 per 100,000 in 2000 to 7.79 per 100,00 in 2009. Those numbers have fluctuated in the years between though, and the 10-year low was in 2007.

"We don't know about 2009 to 2011," said Madelyn Gould, a professor of clinical epidemiology in psychiatry at Columbia who studies youth suicide and prevention efforts. "But probably, the accessibility of the Internet has made it such that there are many more stories about suicide, not necessarily more suicides." Since January of 2010, the words bullying and suicide have appeared together in 592 articles—and that's only print newspapers.

"I would just hope that these stories also talk about the other risks involved with suicidal behavior," said Gould. "If someone is being bullied, they should not jump to the conclusion that one of [their] options is suicide. What they should jump to is, one of the options I have is to get help."

Megan Meier killed herself in 2006 after a cruel MySpace prank orchestrated by an adult neighbor. Her mother, Tina Meier, argues that the pros of linking bullying and suicide still outweigh the cons. "I think since Megan's story there has been a lot more awareness," she explained. "Before, everybody was kind of like, 'Okay, well kids get bullied and we'll deal with it.' We didn't realize the impact that it truly has."

Young people may not be able to avoid exposure to bullying or suicide, but David Litts, an associate director with the Suicide Prevention Resource Center, said parents should take these tragic stories as an opportunity to talk to their children, especially if [they are] already concerned.

"You really need to open up the dialogue in a way that he or she can risk being honest," said Litts. "To look someone in the eye and say, 'Yes, I want to kill myself,' is a hard thing to do. So it's important that whoever asks the question asks it in a way that conveys they're ready to hear an honest answer."

5

Native American Youth Face an Increased Risk of Suicide

Dolores Subia BigFoot

Dolores Subia BigFoot, a trained child psychologist, is the director of Project Making Medicine and the Indian Country Child Trauma Center at the University of Oklahoma Health Sciences Center.

American Indian and Alaska Native (AI/AN) youth living in the United States are particularly vulnerable to child mistreatment, family violence, trauma, and mental and behavioral health problems, all of which can sometimes lead to suicide. In fact, suicide was the second leading cause of death in 2006 for AI/AN individuals between the ages of ten and thirty-four years old. The high prevalence of suicide among the AI/AN communities is due in part to a lack of funding to provide health programs and services. Better mental health care and suicide prevention programs are vital to support the AI/AN population and improve their capacity to fulfill the needs of its youth.

Editor's Note: The 7th Generation Promise: Indian Youth Suicide Prevention Act of 2009 was introduced in the US Senate on August 6, 2009, but died in committee and was not enacted.

Chairman [Byron] Dorgan, Ranking Member [John] Barrasso, and members of the [Senate] Committee [on Indian Affairs], please allow me to express appreciation for the

Dolores Subia BigFoot, "Written Statement of Dolores Subia BigFoot, Ph.D. Director, Indian Country Child Trauma Center and Project Making Medicine University of Oklahoma Health Sciences Center On Behalf of the American Psychological Association Before the Senate Committee on Indian Affairs on The 7th Generation Promise: Indian Youth Suicide Prevention Act of 2009," September 10, 2009. American Psychological Association.

opportunity to speak on behalf of the 150,000 members and affiliates of the American Psychological Association. My name is Dr. Dolores Subia BigFoot and I bring good will from the Caddo Nation of Oklahoma in which I am enrolled and from the Northern Cheyenne Tribe in Montana in which my children are enrolled. I am a child psychologist by training and have devoted 35 years to addressing health disparities in its many forms within our Tribal Nations. Thank you for convening this important hearing to discuss the need to reduce, eliminate, and reveal the devastation of suicide with our American Indian and Alaska Native (AI/AN) youth through the development of federal legislation.

As Director of Project Making Medicine and the Indian Country Child Trauma Center at the University of Oklahoma Health Sciences Center, I profoundly understand the need for safety among our AI/AN youth. There are many diligent and dedicated people who are concerned and working to address this same need for safety, and to provide appropriate mental health and other culturally appropriate interventions that can help prevent suicide. Project Making Medicine is funded by the Office of Child Abuse and Neglect, Children's Bureau, and the Indian Country Child Trauma Center was funded from 2003–2007 by the Substance Abuse and Mental Health Services Administration's (SAMHSA) National Child Traumatic Stress Network. We currently remain a very active affiliate member of this Network, which is an important congressional initiative that works to raise the standard of care for traumatized children and families. It is also important to acknowledge the critical role of SAMHSA's Youth Suicide Prevention and Early Intervention Programs created under the *Garrett Lee Smith Memorial Act*.

The Statistics Regarding Suicide Among Native Americans

Physical, mental, and behavioral health problems continue to affect the AI/AN communities at alarming rates. I am particularly concerned about the disproportionately high prevalence of mental and behavioral health problems among our nation's AI/AN population, including suicide and suicidal ideation. The statistics regarding suicide in the AI/AN communities are astonishing. Research indicates that American Indians account for nearly 11 percent of total suicides in the United States. The suicide rates among youth are also deeply tragic. Of the approximately five million people who are classified as AI or AN in our country, 1.2 million are under the age of 18, which comprises 27 percent of this group. This is particularly significant because in 2006, suicide was the second leading cause of death for AI/AN individuals between the ages of 10 and 34. Furthermore, among AI/AN youth attending Bureau of Indian Affairs schools in 2001, 16 percent had attempted suicide in the 12 months preceding the Youth Risk Behavior Survey.

From 1999 to 2004, AI/AN males between the ages of 15 to 24 had the highest rates of suicide as compared to other age or ethnic groups, 27.99 per 100,000. This age group accounts for 64 percent of all AI/AN suicides. Unfortunately, more than half of all persons who die by suicide in AI/AN communities were never seen by a mental health provider.

These youth often make the decision to take their own lives because they feel a lack of safety in their environment.

Mr. Chairman, as I am sure you know given your steadfast commitment to addressing this tragic problem, high suicide rates have a significant impact on siblings, peers, family members, and communities as a whole.

It is also important to acknowledge the cultural aspects associated with suicide in our AI/AN communities. While progress has been slow in understanding suicide from a cultural perspective, we know that both the historical and current traumatic stressors in Indian Country affect our youth.

The self harm responses that they may exhibit are much like those of other individuals exposed to collective trauma, such as service members/veterans, prisoners of war, and first responders (e.g., firefighters, police officers).

Why Native American Youth Are Vulnerable

Despite the challenges facing our AI/AN communities, we remain optimistic and hopeful. The National Congress of American Indians, along with Tribes and the Indian Health Service, has been formulating best practices related to suicide prevention that will help our youth. These efforts focus on developing a better understanding of what would lead youth to consider suicide. While we know that suicide typically occurs as a single individual act, suicide cannot be understood in isolation. Instead, we must consider a variety of precipitating factors, including child maltreatment, family violence, mental health problems, trauma, loss, grief, and pain that are associated with feelings of hopelessness and a lack of safety among our youth.

The unfortunate and often forgotten reality is that there is an epidemic of violence and harm directed towards this very vulnerable population. AI/AN children and youth experience an increased risk of multiple victimizations. Their capacity to function and to regroup before the next emotional or physical assault diminishes with each missed opportunity to intervene. These youth often make the decision to take their own lives because they feel a lack of safety in their environment. Our youth are in desperate need of safe homes, safe families, and safe communities.

Chronic underfunding of tribal community programs and a lack of infrastructure and human resources create barriers for AI/AN youth. We must provide appropriate resources and opportunities to immediately empower and support our population to build their capacity to address the needs of our youth. Currently, there are an insufficient number of psychologists and other mental health providers of Indigenous heritage. Two vital federal initiatives in place to help address this problem are the Indians Into Psychology Program and the Minority Fellowship Program, funded by the Indian Health Service and SAMHSA, respectively. These programs have a strong history of success and are critical to building the ethnic minority pipeline. As such, it is important that increased funding is provided to these initiatives to meet the current mental and behavioral health needs of our population. At the same time, while we work to build a sufficient professional workforce, tribal communities require immediate and innovative resources to meet the urgent needs of our youth and families.

At the University of Oklahoma Health Sciences Center, we are currently utilizing a video conferencing system through the internet in which we are training via real time mental health providers in tribal communities in Washington State. In the past, we have trained via internet tribal providers located in Alaska, California, Utah, and across Oklahoma. The National Child Traumatic Stress Network is also developing a sophisticated distance learning system that can help providers access the specific training they need when working with AI/AN youth and families. I strongly recommend the continued support and expansion of the National Child Traumatic Stress Network as an important resource to ensure that we have a national infrastructure of child trauma experts and providers who can help to meet the diverse needs of our youth.

This past June [2009], we traveled to Anchorage, Alaska to provide a Mental Health First Aid training for individuals from the villages or Native corporations who were interested in developing basic skills in assisting those experiencing mental or behavioral health problems, including suicide risk. Unfortunately many village providers and other village helpers who expressed interest in the training were unable to attend given the lack of transportation resources. With telehealth capability, such barriers might be overcome to enable the delivery of critical mental health and suicide prevention education and training in remote or less accessible areas and to large groups of community members.

We appreciate your efforts in developing the *7th Generation Promise: Indian Youth Suicide Prevention Act of 2009*. This legislation aims to increase and enhance the provision of mental health care to AI/AN youth by decreasing disparities in access and improving quality of mental health care. We look forward to working with Congress, the Indian Health Service, the Children's Bureau, and SAMHSA as this proposal moves through the legislative process.

Mr. Chairman, Ranking Member, and members of the Committee, I am honored, my family is honored, and my tribe is honored by this invitation to join you here today. The American Psychological Association and the psychology community look forward to continuing to work with you and the tribal communities to ensure that our youth receive the mental and behavioral health care that they urgently need and deserve.

6

Cultural Programs Will Combat Suicide Among Native American Youth

Mary Annette Pember

Mary Annette Pember, a member of the Red Cliff Band of the Wisconsin Ojibwe, is a journalist who focuses on Native American issues and culture.

The American Indian population has a unique decades-long history of trauma and loss—loss of their land and loss of their culture. This history may help explain the high rate of mental illness exhibited in this population, along with the ensuing alcoholism, substance abuse, and suicide ideology. For example, the suicide rate for American Indians and Alaska natives is more than double that of other ethnic groups nationwide. In efforts to lower these rates, mental health researchers have found that suicide prevention programs that acknowledge and incorporate cultural traditions and values result in an increase of American Indian youth willing to seek help and a decrease in suicide and suicide attempts.

On Nov. 13, 2008, 14-year-old Jami Jetty of the Dakota tribe hanged herself from her bunk bed in her family's home on the Spirit Lake Reservation in North Dakota.

Mary Annette Pember, "Fighting the Suicide Spirit: Tribal Colleges Are at the Forefront of Communitywide Effort to Combat Suicide with Culturally Relevant Methods," *Diverse Issues in Higher Education*, vol. 27, no. 21, November 25, 2010, p. 14. Copyright © 2010 by Cox, Matthews & Associates, Inc. All rights reserved. Reproduced by permission.

Weeks after the funeral, when her mother, Cora Whiteman-Tiger, returned to work as an executive assistant for the tribal council, she found a flier on her desk from Wiconi Ohitika, the suicide-prevention program at Cankdeska Cikana Community College. The flier was an invitation to a "Wiping of the Tears" ceremony and sweat lodge for those who lost loved ones to suicide.

"I was standing there (at the ceremony) with an open wound," she recalls. Through the community ceremony, she says, she received messages of comfort and hope from her daughter.

Addressing the Cumulative Historical Trauma

"She told me I should let others know that suicide is not the way to go; it's really scary. She said the lost spirits of those who committed suicide wander around crying and that we should pray for them," Whiteman-Tiger says.

With the help of Wiconi Ohitika, which means "Strong Life" in the Dakota language, Whiteman-Tiger has taken Jami's message to the community through prayer circles, public service announcements and youth dances.

Suicide-prevention strategies must recognize American Indians' unique history and needs to be effective.

Whiteman-Tiger's experience exemplifies the successful elements of an American Indian suicide-prevention program. Connection with community and her culture empowered her to speak out about suicide and has led to a healing experience for her and the community at large.

The Wiconi Ohitika project is one of several tribal college and mainstream university efforts to address the high rates of suicide among American Indians. According to the U.S. Centers for Disease Control and Prevention, the suicide rate for

47

American Indians and Alaska natives is more than twice the national average for other ethnic groups. It is the second-leading cause of death behind unintentional injuries and accidents for Indian youth aged 15 to 24.

The complex reasons behind these statistics dictate that suicide-prevention strategies must recognize American Indians' unique history and needs to be effective, say American Indian mental health providers and researchers.

American Indians experience cumulative trauma across generations resulting from the historical loss of land, culture, family and self-esteem, according to Dr. Jacqueline Gray, an assistant professor at the University of North Dakota (UND) Center for Rural Health at the School of Medicine. The response to this historical trauma is mental illness, alcoholism, substance abuse and suicide.

"This stripping away of culture and land has resulted in a hole in the heart that we may not be able to identify as historical trauma but we experience nonetheless," says Gray, president-elect of the Society of Indian Psychologists and member of the Choctaw and Cherokee tribes.

The "contagion effect," in which incidents of suicide increase among those in small, often isolated reservation communities following a peer's suicide, is a big factor in American Indian suicide rates.

Research findings from the Substance Abuse and Mental Health Services Administration (SAMHSA) also indicate that mental health services are not easily accessible to American Indians and Alaskan natives because of a lack of funding, shortage of culturally appropriate services and the high turnover of mental health professionals. This explains why Indians underuse mental health services and discontinue therapy.

Overall, according to SAMHSA, 90 percent of the 30,000 people who die annually by suicide have a diagnosable mental illness and/or substance-abuse disorder. National Violent Death Reporting System data indicate that one-third of all suicide victims tested positive for alcohol and nearly one in five had evidence of opiates. According to Gray, 90 percent of American Indians who committed suicide were under the influence of drugs or alcohol.

Engaging the Community and Incorporating Cultural Traditions

In her research, Gray found that successful suicide-prevention programming among American Indian and Alaskan native populations must address these underlying causes using culturally appropriate means. Gray says she and other mental health researchers have found overwhelmingly that the preservation or reclaiming of cultural heritage is associated with a lower prevalence of suicide attempts among American Indians and Alaskan natives.

Young American Indians who are more culturally and spiritually connected exhibit fewer suicidal tendencies and greater resistance to stress.

Such suicide-prevention programming should engage all members of the community in order to ensure strong community ownership, says Antonette Halsey of the Dakota tribe, vice president of library and community services at CCCC [Cankdeska Cikana Community College] and coordinator of the Wiconi Ohitika project. Wiconi Ohitika calls on community spiritual leaders and elders to help teach traditional Dakota beading, regalia and star quilt making, singing and traditional food preparation. These classes provide a natural venue to share the values of Dakota heritage while allowing students and elders to form relationships. Open to students and the reservation community at large, the classes are not exclusively suicide-prevention programming but incorporate anti-suicide information in the course curriculum.

"There is a hunger among our young people for our traditional ways," says Halsey. Unlike mainstream approaches, which typically include public service announcements and require people in crisis to reach out to mental health professionals, programs geared toward American Indians should offer the same anti-suicide message but as part of a cultural activity and include respected American Indian leaders and elders who can engage students on a one-on-one basis, experts say.

This approach is in keeping with research findings described in the article, "Circle of Strength: A Case Description of Culturally Integrated Suicide Prevention Programming," co-written by Gray and Dr. Jennifer Muehlenkamp, a UND psychologist, and published in the *Archives of Suicide Research* in April [2010]. The authors found that by engaging the community and incorporating cultural traditions, a tribal college can ensure its students will seek help when they need it. Researchers have also found that young American Indians who are more culturally and spiritually connected exhibit fewer suicidal tendencies and greater resistance to stress.

Tribal colleges and some traditionally White institutions use a variety of suicide-prevention protocols in their programming but all share the common approach of including the community and networking for resources from mainstream and tribal sources.

Teaching Culturally Appropriate Suicide-Prevention Programs

UND's American Indian Campus Suicide Prevention Program, for example, partners with reservations and tribal colleges to provide comprehensive services to students, and staff may refer UND students seeking more traditional healing practices, as opposed to therapy, to an appropriate tribal person.

Nebraska Indian Community College began offering a suicide-prevention counseling certificate program last year.

Graduates will be qualified to work under the supervision of a licensed mental health practitioner.

The College of Menominee Nation incorporates the "Question, Persuade, Refer" [QPR] protocol into its Natamatowak "They Help Each Other" suicide-prevention programming. QPR is presented as an emergency life-saving device for those at risk for suicide. According to information from the QPR Institute, people can be trained to recognize the warning signs of suicide crisis and how to refer someone for help.

The Wiconi Ohitika project uses the QPR protocol as well as the Sources of Strength model originally developed for rural and tribal communities. The model uses teams of peer leaders mentored by adult advisers to change peer social norms about seeking help. It promotes and focuses on connectivity, bonding and peer adult partnership and help-seeking behaviors.

Cooperation exemplifies the Dakota way of life in which people must respect the gift of life and accept the responsibility to live in harmony with each other and the earth.

Dr. Cynthia Lindquist of the Dakota tribe, president of Cankdeska Cikana Community College, says the most significant component of Wiconi Ohitika is working together.

According to Lindquist, cooperation exemplifies the Dakota way of life in which people must respect the gift of life and accept the responsibility to live in harmony with each other and the earth.

"Tribal colleges have as their core mission the teaching and learning of indigenous culture and language. Since this is rooted in spirituality, we are mobilizing all the spiritual leaders of the reservation and encouraging our families to believe and practice some form of faith and worship," says Lindquist.

A resistance to confronting suicide lingers in the community, says Whiteman-Tiger.

"But we have to talk about it. I will keep talking and fighting that spirit that took my baby until I can't fight anymore. That was my promise to the grandfathers in the lodge."

7

Volatile Mix: Kids at Risk for Suicide Can Get Guns

Maggie Fox

Maggie Fox is a senior writer for NBC News.

Various studies that covered many cities and states in the United States found a strong link between completed suicides and the presence of firearms in homes. This is an alarming correlation and this higher risk of suicide pertains to guns in the home regardless of how the guns are stored. Almost half of all completed suicides involve firearms in the United States.

As many as one in five children who are at risk of suicide live in homes where they can get hold of guns—the single most effective means to killing themselves—researchers reported on Monday.

They said their findings show it's extremely important to screen children for suicide risk, and to educate parents about how to keep guns out of their hands if they are. And early treatment is also vital.

The researchers, who presented their findings at the Pediatric Academic Societies meeting in Washington, D.C., say they don't want their results to get mixed up in the current debate over firearms regulation. They just want to keep kids safe.

"A lot of kids, surprisingly, don't have a history of mental illness but they attempt suicide," says Dr. Stephen Teach, an emergency room doctor at Children's National Medical Center in Washington, D.C.

Suicide is the No. 3 cause of death for children and youths aged 10 to 24, according to the Centers for Disease Control and Prevention. About 4,600 kids and young adults kill themselves each year, and 45 percent of them use guns. Another 40 percent suffocate or strangle themselves and 8 percent poison themselves.

"Guns are the most lethal method that is commonly used in suicide attempts," says Dr. Matt Miller, an injury control expert at the Harvard School of Public Health. People who try to commit suicide using pills or by cutting themselves complete the suicide just 3 percent of the time, he said.

Teach and colleagues made their discovery while trying to come up with an easy, short questionnaire for emergency room doctors to use while seeing children for a range of troubles. Their study included 524 patients ages 10 to 21 being seen at three pediatric emergency rooms.

"When we were asking kids these questions, we also asked kids questions about firearms and bullets. To our surprise, one-fifth reported firearms in the home," Teach said in an interview. "That's a pretty volatile mix. Nearly half of all completed suicides involve firearms, which is pretty scary."

They found 151 of the kids, or 29 percent of them, were at risk for suicide, and 17 percent of them reported guns in or around the home. Of those at risk for suicide and who knew guns were in their home, 31 percent knew how to get the guns, 31 percent knew how to find the bullets, and 15 percent knew how to access both the guns and the bullets.

Other studies show that suicide is usually an impulsive act. If a person tries but fails to commit suicide, he or she is unlikely to try again. So taking away a quick and lethal method could save many lives.

One in 10 kids who were not in the emergency department for psychiatric complaints also screened positive for suicide risk. "It is frighteningly common in this age group," Teach said.

So, number one, says Teach—it's important to identify children who might be thinking about suicide. "Once you identify the kids, be willing to engage in a conversation about access to firearms," he said.

The four questions are simple:

- In the past few weeks, have you wished you were dead?

- In the past few weeks, have you felt that you or your family would be better off if you were dead?

- In the past week, have you been having thoughts about killing yourself?

- Have you ever tried to kill yourself?

"It works. It identifies the kids (at risk)," Teach said. He says the conversation does not seem to put ideas into the kids' heads.

Suicide rates overall are much higher in states with higher gun ownership.

"What we found, to our surprise, was that kids really want to be asked," he said. "The reactions were positive. They said, 'I am glad you asked.'"

The key signs for parents to look for: Withdrawal from friends, substance abuse, differences in performance in school, changing their group of friends, says Teach. Changes in appetite, dropping hobbies, and just appearing sad are also warning signs.

"If you feel sad around your kids, it may be a sign," he said. "If they bum you out, they are probably bummed out."

Such conversations are very difficult, Teach said. "This is on the list of hard things to talk about, like sex and drugs," he said. "It's all dialogue, dialogue, dialogue. Don't be afraid to ask."

And if kids are at risk, they need to be kept safe from guns, pediatricians at the meeting agreed. "Between 1999 and 2010 there were 22,193 suicides among children 5 to 19," Miller said.

Miller says suicide rates overall are much higher in states with higher gun ownership.

"Where there are more guns in the United States, there are more people dying," he told a session at the meeting.

He said people with guns need to learn more about how to protect their children from them.

"There are 300 million firearms in civilian hands in the United States," Miller said. He said the latest statistics showed 1.5 million children lived in homes with loaded and unlocked guns.

The issue can be political, but Teach is clear he does not want to get into a political argument about gun ownership. "This is not really a story about who has guns. The issue is a significant proportion of kids at risk for suicide have access to firearms," Teach said.

8

Gay Teens Face an Increased Risk of Suicide

Randy Dotinga

Randy Dotinga is a reporter with almost a decade of experience. His articles have won many awards, including first place for news reporting from the California Newspaper Publishers Association.

Lesbian, gay, and bisexual (LGB) youth as a group experience more suicidal behavior than other youth, largely because LGB youth generally have more severe risk factors and fewer protective factors in their lives than heterosexual youth. For example, various studies have shown that LGB youth are more likely to have experienced discrimination and stigma in their social environment. Furthermore, LGB youth often lack important protective factors, such as family or religious support. These stressors are associated with mental illness, isolation, substance abuse, and harmful relationships with family, peers, and community—all of which put them at an increased risk for suicide.

Students targeted because they're believed to be gay—as many as one in seven young teens—are much more likely than others to be suicidal and depressed, a new survey finds.

More than 10 percent of eighth-grade boys and girls reported that they're victimized because of perceived sexual orientation, according to a large survey of students in Washington state.

"It has a profound impact on their quality of life and the way they think of themselves," said Donald Patrick, a professor of health services at the University of Washington in Seattle. "Those in eighth grade are in a particularly vulnerable position."

These children "feel alone in life, that they don't feel as good as other people and their self-esteem is highly affected," Patrick said.

The survey results, published online May 16 [2013] in the *American Journal of Public Health*, don't offer insight into whether bullying contributes to depression and suicidal thoughts in its victims. It's possible that kids with existing mental illnesses may be more likely to be bullied and perceived as gay.

Nor does the research establish a clear cause-and-effect relationship between bullying and suicidal thoughts. But Patrick said "it's clear that there's an association, and I wouldn't be so worried about the causation." Prior research has also suggested that gay, lesbian, bisexual and transgender children are more likely to be suicidal and hurt themselves.

---

26 percent of male 12th-graders targeted for being perceived as gay said they had been suicidal within the past year.

A string of teen suicides in 2010—including the death of Rutgers University freshman Tyler Clementi—put the issue in the public eye. Syndicated columnist Dan Savage launched a campaign called "It Gets Better" to give hope to gay teens that their lives will improve. Participants have included numerous celebrities and politicians, including President Barack Obama.

Based on the new findings, bully-prevention programs must address kids picked on because of their sexual orientation, the study authors said.

The study is based on a 2010 survey of nearly 28,000 students in grades eight, 10 and 12. Among boys, 14 percent of eighth-graders, 11 percent of 10th-graders and 9 percent of 12th-graders reported being bullied within the previous month because they were thought to be gay. The numbers were 11 percent, 10 percent and 6 percent, respectively, for girls.

The survey defined bullying based on sexual orientation as being "bullied, harassed or intimidated at school" because they were thought to be gay or bisexual. It defined other types of bullying as when one or more students "say or do nasty or unpleasant things" to another person or tease someone "repeatedly in a way he or she finds offensive." In most cases, more students reported being bullied for other reasons.

Compared to kids bullied for other reasons or not bullied at all, those targeted because they were perceived to be gay were much more likely to have considered suicide in the past year, to have been depressed in the past year and to say they don't feel good about themselves.

For example, 26 percent of male 12th-graders targeted for being perceived as gay said they had been suicidal within the past year, compared to 8 percent of those not bullied. The rate also was more than three times greater for female seniors.

Brian Mustanski, an associate professor in the department of medical social sciences at the Northwestern University Feinberg School of Medicine, in Chicago, said the survey has some strengths but fails to ask whether those bullied are actually gay and not just perceived to be.

"Because of this, it is a major underestimate of the rate of bullying among gay youth," he said.

Mustanski agreed with Patrick that teachers and school leaders need to promote comfortable and safe environments. "While family and peer support have important positive effects for gay youth and reduce feelings of suicide and depression, you cannot 'support away' these toxic effects of bullying," he said.

"Schools and communities need to put in place policies and practices that make schools and neighborhoods safe for all kids," he said.

9

Teens with Asperger's Syndrome May Attempt Suicide

Tony Attwood

Tony Attwood is a psychologist who lives in Queensland, Australia, and is the author of several books on Asperger's syndrome.

Young people with Asperger's syndrome have difficulty fitting in with their peers. They lack typical social skills—such as the ability to engage in standard conversations or to feel empathy for others—and are prone to experience intense emotions and heightened sensory perceptions. Because of their nonconformity, these adolescents often are victims of bullying, ridicule, and rejection, and can end up feeling isolated and misunderstood. As a result, people with Asperger's syndrome sometimes turn to suicide as an escape from the emotional stress and frustration that fills their lives.

Perhaps the simplest way to understand Asperger's syndrome is to think of it as describing someone who perceives and thinks about the world differently to other people.

Although clinicians have only recently described these differences, the unusual profile of abilities that we define as Asperger's syndrome has probably been an important and valuable characteristic of our species throughout evolution. It was not until the late twentieth century that we had a name to describe such individuals. We currently use the diagnostic term Asperger's syndrome, based on the remarkably perceptive descriptions of Dr Hans Asperger, a Viennese paediatrician, who, in 1944, noticed that some of the children referred to his clinic had very similar personality characteristics and behaviour. . . .

Recognizing Characteristics of Asperger's Syndrome

Asperger was clearly entranced by children with autistic personality disorder and he wrote a remarkably perceptive description of the children's difficulties and abilities. He observed that the children's social maturity and social reasoning were delayed and some aspects of their social abilities were quite unusual at any stage of development. The children had difficulty making friends and they were often teased by other children. There were impairments in verbal and non-verbal communication, especially the conversational aspects of language. The children's use of language was pedantic, and some children had an unusual prosody that affected the tone, pitch and rhythm of speech. The grammar and vocabulary may have been relatively advanced but, at the end of the conversation, one had the impression that there was something unusual about their ability to have the typical conversation that would be expected with children of that age. Asperger also observed and described conspicuous impairments in the communication and control of emotions, and a tendency to intellectualize feelings. Empathy was not as mature as one would expect, considering the children's intellectual abilities. The children also had an egocentric preoccupation with a specific topic or interest that would dominate their thoughts and time. Some of the children had difficulty maintaining attention in class and had specific learning problems. Asperger noted that they often needed more assistance with self-help and organizational skills from their mothers than one would expect. He described conspicuous clumsiness in terms of gait and coordination. He also noted that some children were extremely sensitive to particular sounds, aromas, textures and touch.

Social phobia, or social anxiety disorder, would be expected to be relatively common for those with Asperger's syndrome, especially in the teenage and adult years.

Asperger considered that the characteristics could be identified in some children as young as two to three years, although for other children, the characteristics only became conspicuous some years later. He also noticed that some of the parents, especially the fathers of such children, appeared to share some of the personality characteristics of their child. He wrote that the condition was probably due to genetic or neurological, rather than psychological or environmental, factors. . . .

If a parent has a mood disorder, a child with Asperger's syndrome could have a genetic predisposition to strong emotions. This may be one of the factors that explain problems with the intensity and management of emotions that are characteristics of Asperger's syndrome. However, there are other factors. When one considers the inevitable difficulties people with Asperger's syndrome have with regard to social reasoning, empathy, conversation skills, a different learning style and heightened sensory perception, they are clearly prone to considerable stress, anxiety, frustration and emotional exhaustion. They are also prone to being rejected by peers and frequently being teased and bullied, which can lead to low self-esteem and feeling depressed. During adolescence, there can be an increasing awareness of a lack of social success, and greater insight into being different to other people—another factor in the development of a reactive depression. Thus, there may be genetic and environmental factors that explain the higher incidence of mood disorders. . . .

Teens with Asperger's Often Feel Like Social Outcasts

Social phobia, or social anxiety disorder, would be expected to be relatively common for those with Asperger's syndrome, especially in the teenage and adult years when they are more acutely aware of their confusion in social situations, of making social mistakes, and possibly suffering ridicule. A typical person who develops social phobia is very concerned as to what others will think of him or her, with a fear of being embarrassed. I have noted that young people with Asperger's syndrome who develop signs of social phobia are more avoidant of self-criticism than the criticism of others, and have a pathological fear of making a social mistake. Treatment includes medication and CBT [cognitive behavior therapy], but someone with Asperger's syndrome who has social phobia will also need guidance in improving social skills, and encouragement to be less self-critical and to cope with social mistakes.

Depression

Our psychological and biological models of mood disorders suggest a continuum between long-standing anxiety and depression. When anxious, the person thinks 'What if X happens?' But in depression, the person assumes the worst outcome is unavoidable. It is interesting that anxiety and depressive disorders both respond positively to the same medications and CBT.

There are a number of characteristics of depression: physical and mental exhaustion; feeling sad or empty; and having little interest in previously pleasurable experiences. There can be social withdrawal, a change in appetite with either weight gain or loss, and a change in sleep pattern with little, or excessive, sleep. The person talks about feeling worthless and guilty, is unable to concentrate, and may have thoughts about death.

Some of the characteristics of Asperger's syndrome can prolong the duration and increase the intensity of depression.

People with Asperger's syndrome appear vulnerable to feeling depressed, with about one in three children and adults having a clinical depression. The reasons for people with Asperger's syndrome to be depressed are many and include the long-term consequences on self-esteem of feeling unaccepted and misunderstood, the mental exhaustion from trying to succeed socially, feelings of loneliness, being tormented, teased, bullied and ridiculed by peers, and a cognitive style that is pessimistic, focusing on what could go wrong. I have listened to adolescents with Asperger's syndrome who are clinically depressed and often heard the comment, 'I feel I don't belong.' The depression can lead to a severe withdrawal from social contact and thoughts that, without social success, there is no point in life.

People with Asperger's syndrome are often perfectionists, tend to be exceptionally good at noticing mistakes, and have a conspicuous fear of failure. There can be a relative lack of optimism, with a tendency to expect failure and not to be able to control events. As the adolescent with Asperger's syndrome achieves greater intellectual maturity, this can be associated with an increased insight into being different and self-perception of being irreparably defective and socially stupid.

People with Asperger's Communicate in Unconventional Ways

Some of the characteristics of Asperger's syndrome can prolong the duration and increase the intensity of depression. The person with Asperger's syndrome may not disclose his or her inner feelings, preferring to retreat into solitude, avoiding conversation (especially when the conversation is about feelings and experiences), and trying to resolve the depression by subjective thought. Typical people are better at, and more confident about, disclosing feelings and knowing that another person may provide a more objective opinion and act as an emotional restorative. Family and friends of a typical person may be able to temporarily halt, and to a certain extent alleviate, the mood by words and gestures of reassurance and affection. They may be able to distract the person who is depressed by initiating enjoyable experiences, or using humour. These emotional rescue strategies are sometimes less effective for people with Asperger's syndrome, who try to solve personal and practical issues by themselves and for whom affection and compassion may not be as effective an emotional restorative.

Clinical experience confirms that some adolescents and adults with Asperger's syndrome who are clinically depressed can consider suicide as a means of ending the emotional pain and despair.

The signs of depression can be the same as would be expected of typical children and adults, but clinicians who specialize in Asperger's syndrome have noted another feature that can be indicative of depression. The special interest of the person with Asperger's syndrome is often associated with pleasure and the acquisition of knowledge about the physical rather than the social world. However, when the person becomes depressed the interest can become morbid, and the person preoccupied with aspects of death.

Sometimes the reason for the change in the focus of the interest to the macabre can be mystifying, but is the child's attempt to communicate confusion, sadness and uncertainty about what to do. In her book on autism and Asperger's syndrome, Pat Howlin described Joshua, whose father was a news cameraman on war assignment. His father was missing for several days and the family was extremely worried. Joshua began asking his mother incessant questions about the weapons used by each side, and how many people were being killed. During this time of anxiety for the family, Joshua did not express worry or seek comfort from family members. On his father's return, he wanted to know how many dead bodies he had photographed. When Joshua was asked about his apparent lack of concern or compassion, he said that he was aware that his mother and sister were upset but he was unable to reassure them since he did not know what had happened to his father, and he did not want to tell a lie—he did not know what to say. His morbid interest and questions were actually 'a cry for help', and his attempt to try to communicate and understand his own feelings. Parents and clinicians may need to look beyond the focus of the interest and recognize a mood disorder (anxiety or depression) that is being expressed in an unconventional way, but a way that may be expected in someone who has difficulty understanding and expressing emotions.

Clinical experience confirms that some adolescents and adults with Asperger's syndrome who are clinically depressed can consider suicide as a means of ending the emotional pain and despair. The person carefully plans a means of suicide over days or weeks. However, children and some adolescents with Asperger's syndrome can experience what I describe as a 'suicide attack', a spur-of-the-moment decision to make a dramatic end to life. Liliana, an adult with Asperger's syndrome, conceptualized her intense depression as a 'soul migraine'. We recognize the occurrence of a panic attack in typical people, which can occur very quickly and be unanticipated; the person has a sudden and overwhelming feeling of anxiety. In a depression attack, the person with Asperger's syndrome has a sudden and overwhelming feeling of depression and there can be an impulsive and dramatic attempt at suicide. The child can suddenly run in front of a moving vehicle or go to a bridge to jump from a height to end his or her life. Those who have been with the person may not have identified any conspicuous preceding depressive thoughts, but a minor irritation, such as being teased or making a mistake, can trigger an intense emotional reaction, a depression attack. The person can be restrained and prevented from injury, and remarkably, a short while later, usually returns to his or her typical emotional state, which is not indicative of a severe clinical depression. . . .

Managing the Emotions of People with Asperger's Syndrome

When a mood disorder is diagnosed in a child or adult with Asperger's syndrome, the clinical psychologist or psychiatrist will need to know how to modify psychological treatments for mood disorders to accommodate the unusual cognitive profile of people with Asperger's syndrome. The primary psychological treatment for mood disorders is Cognitive Behaviour Therapy (CBT), which has been developed and refined over several decades. Research studies have established that CBT is an effective treatment to change the way a person thinks about and responds to emotions such as anxiety, sadness and anger. CBT focuses on the maturity, complexity, subtlety and vocabulary of emotions, and dysfunctional or illogical thinking and incorrect assumptions. Thus, it has direct applicability to children and adults with Asperger's syndrome who have impaired or delayed Theory of Mind abilities and difficulty understanding, expressing and managing emotions. The theoretical model of emotions used in CBT is consistent with current scientific models of human emotions, namely becoming more consciously aware of one's emotional state, knowing how to respond to the emotion, and becoming more sensitive to how others are feeling. We now have published case studies and objective scientific evidence that CBT does significantly reduce mood disorders in children and adults with Asperger's syndrome. . . .

Medication is often prescribed for children and adults with Asperger's syndrome to manage emotions. If the child or adult is showing clear signs of a mood disorder then medication is recommended as an emotion management tool. Clinical experience has confirmed the value of medication for the treatment of anxiety, depression and anger in children and adults with Asperger's syndrome but there are some concerns often voiced by parents and those with Asperger's syndrome. One concern of parents and physicians is that, at present, we do not have longitudinal studies of the long-term effect of psychotropic medication on young children with Asperger's syndrome. However, there is evidence that low doses of such medication can benefit some adults with Asperger's syndrome. . . .

People with Asperger's syndrome clearly have problems understanding emotions within themselves and others, and expressing emotions at an appropriate level for the situation. We now have strategies to help people with Asperger's syndrome to learn about emotions, and effective psychological treatment for any secondary mood disorder. Unfortunately, typical people have difficulty empathizing with such experiences, and can only imagine what it must be like to live in a world of powerful emotions that are confusing and overwhelming. Liliana, an adult with Asperger's syndrome, explained one of the reasons people with Asperger's syndrome may lead an emotionally reclusive life when she said to me, 'We don't have emotional skin or protection. We are exposed, and that is why we hide.'

10

Monitored Antidepressant Use Can Help Prevent Teen Suicide

National Institute of Mental Health

The National Institute of Mental Health (NIMH) is part of the National Institutes of Health (NIH), a component of the US Department of Health and Human Services. The mission of NIMH is to transform the understanding and treatment of mental illnesses through basic and clinical research, paving the way for prevention, recovery, and cure.

It is estimated that 5 percent of adolescents suffer from major depression, many of whom are treated with antidepressant medications known as selective serotonin reuptake inhibitors (SSRIs). Although this type of antidepressant has proven effective for adults, clinical trial results showed that SSRI use might cause suicidal behavior in children and adolescents, thus the US Food and Drug Administration (FDA) issued a public warning in October 2004. Because depression itself is a severe risk factor for suicide, it is difficult to determine whether SSRIs increase suicidal behavior in young people. It is therefore recommended that children who are prescribed SSRIs as medication for depression be carefully monitored for side effects, such as suicidal thinking or behavior.

Depression is a serious disorder that can cause significant problems in mood, thinking, and behavior at home, in school, and with peers. It is estimated that major depressive disorder (MDD) affects about 5 percent of adolescents.

"Antidepressant Medications for Children and Adolescents: Information for Parents and Caregivers," National Institute of Mental Health, last reviewed May 21, 2012.

Research has shown that, as in adults, depression in children and adolescents is treatable. Certain antidepressant medications, called selective serotonin reuptake inhibitors (SSRIs), can be beneficial to children and adolescents with MDD. Certain types of psychological therapies also have been shown to be effective. However, our knowledge of antidepressant treatments in youth, though growing substantially, is limited compared to what we know about treating depression in adults.

What Is the Concern About Antidepressant Use?

Recently, there has been some concern that the use of antidepressant medications themselves may induce suicidal behavior in youths. Following a thorough and comprehensive review of all the available published and unpublished controlled clinical trials of antidepressants in children and adolescents, the U.S. Food and Drug Administration (FDA) issued a public warning in October 2004 about an increased risk of suicidal thoughts or behavior (suicidality) in children and adolescents treated with SSRI antidepressant medications. In 2006, an advisory committee to the FDA recommended that the agency extend the warning to include young adults up to age 25.

SSRI medications usually have few side effects in children and adolescents, but for unknown reasons, they may trigger agitation and abnormal behavior in certain individuals.

More recently, results of a comprehensive review of pediatric trials conducted between 1988 and 2006 suggested that the benefits of antidepressant medications likely outweigh their risks to children and adolescents with major depression and anxiety disorders. The study, partially funded by NIMH

[National Institute of Mental Health], was published in the April 18, 2007, issue of the *Journal of the American Medical Association.*

In the FDA review, no completed suicides occurred among nearly 2,200 children treated with SSRI medications. However, about 4 percent of those taking SSRI medications experienced suicidal thinking or behavior, including actual suicide attempts—twice the rate of those taking placebo, or sugar pills.

In response, the FDA adopted a "black box" label warning indicating that antidepressants may increase the risk of suicidal thinking and behavior in some children and adolescents with MDD. A black-box warning is the most serious type of warning in prescription drug labeling.

The warning also notes that children and adolescents talking SSRI medications should be closely monitored for any worsening in depression, emergence of suicidal thinking or behavior, or unusual changes in behavior, such as sleeplessness, agitation, or withdrawal from normal social situations. Close monitoring is especially important during the first four weeks of treatment. SSRI medications usually have few side effects in children and adolescents, but for unknown reasons, they may trigger agitation and abnormal behavior in certain individuals.

What Do We Know About Antidepressant Medications?

The SSRIs include: fluoxetine (Prozac), sertraline (Zoloft), paroxetine (Paxil), citalopram (Celexa), escitalopram (Lexapro), fluvoxamine (Luvox).

Another antidepressant medication, venlafaxine (Effexor), is not an SSRI but is closely related.

SSRI medications are considered an improvement over older antidepressant medications because they have fewer side effects and are less likely to be harmful if taken in an overdose, which is an issue for patients with depression already at risk for suicide. They have been shown to be safe and effective for adults.

However, use of SSRI medications among children and adolescents ages 10 to 19 has risen dramatically in the past several years. Fluoxetine (Prozac) is the only medication approved by the FDA for use in treating depression in children ages 8 and older. The other SSRI medications and the SSRI-related antidepressant venlafaxine have not been approved for treatment of depression in children or adolescents, but doctors still sometimes prescribe them to children on an "off-label" basis. In June 2003, however, the FDA recommended that paroxetine [Paxil] not be used in children and adolescents for treating MDD.

Fluoxetine can be helpful in treating childhood depression, and can lead to significant improvement of depression overall. However, it may increase the risk for suicidal behaviors *in a small subset of adolescents*. As with all medical decisions, doctors and families should weigh the risks and benefits of treatment for each individual patient.

A child or adolescent with MDD should be carefully and thoroughly evaluated by a doctor to determine if medication is appropriate. Psychotherapy often is tried as an initial treatment for mild depression. Psychotherapy may help to determine the severity and persistence of the depression and whether antidepressant medications may be warranted. Types of psychotherapies include "cognitive behavioral therapy [CBT]," which helps people learn new ways of thinking and behaving, and "interpersonal therapy," which helps people understand and work through troubled personal relationships.

Those who are prescribed an SSRI medication should receive ongoing medical monitoring. Children already taking an SSRI medication should remain on the medication if it has been helpful, but should be carefully monitored by a doctor for side effects. Parents should promptly seek medical advice and evaluation if their child or adolescent experiences suicidal thinking or behavior, nervousness, agitation, irritability, mood instability, or sleeplessness that either emerges or worsens during treatment with SSRI medications.

A combination of medication and psychotherapy is the most effective treatment for adolescents with depression.

Once started, treatment with these medications should not be abruptly stopped. Although they are not habit-forming or addictive, abruptly ending an antidepressant can cause withdrawal symptoms or lead to a relapse. Families should not discontinue treatment without consulting their doctor.

All treatments can be associated with side effects. Families and doctors should carefully weigh the risks and benefits, and maintain appropriate follow-up and monitoring to help control for the risks.

What Does Research Reveal?

An individual's response to a medication cannot be predicted with certainty. It is extremely difficult to determine whether SSRI medications increase the risk for completed suicide, especially because depression itself increases the risk for suicide and because completed suicides, especially among children and adolescents, are rare. Most controlled trials are too small to detect for rare events such as suicide (thousands of participants are needed). In addition, controlled trials typically exclude patients considered at high risk for suicide.

One major clinical trial, the NIMH-funded "Treatment for Adolescents with Depression Study" (TADS), has indicated that a combination of medication and psychotherapy is the most effective treatment for adolescents with depression. The clinical trial of 439 adolescents ages 12 to 17 with MDD compared four treatment groups—one that received a combination of fluoxetine and CBT, one that received fluoxetine only, one that received CBT only, and one that received a placebo only. After the first 12 weeks, 71 percent responded to the combination treatment of fluoxetine and CBT, 61 percent responded to the fluoxetine only treatment, 43 percent responded to the CBT only treatment, and 35 percent responded to the placebo treatment.

At the beginning of the study, 29 percent of the TADS participants were having clinically significant suicidal thoughts. Although the rate of suicidal thinking decreased among all the treatment groups, those in the fluoxetine/CBT combination treatment group showed the greatest reduction in suicidal thinking.

Researchers are working to better understand the relationship between antidepressant medications and suicide. So far, results are mixed. One study, using national Medicaid files, found that among adults, the use of antidepressants does not seem to be related to suicide attempts or deaths. However, the analysis found that the use of antidepressant medications may be related to suicide attempts and deaths among children and adolescents.

Another study analyzed health plan records for 65,103 patients treated for depression. It found no significant increase among adults and young people in the risk for suicide after starting treatment with newer antidepressant medications.

A third study analyzed suicide data from the National Vital Statistics and commercial prescription data. It found that among children ages five to 14, suicide rates from 1996 to 1998 were actually lower in areas of the country with higher rates of SSRI antidepressant prescriptions. The relationship between the suicide rates and the SSRI use rates, however, is unclear.

New NIMH-funded research will help clarify the complex interplay between suicide and antidepressant medications. In addition, the NIMH-funded "Treatment of Resistant Depression in Adolescents" (TORDIA) study, will investigate how best to treat adolescents whose depression is resistant to the first SSRI medication they have tried. Finally, NIMH also is supporting the "Treatment of Adolescent Suicide Attempters" (TASA) study, which is investigating the treatment of adolescents who have attempted suicide. Treatments include antidepressant medications, CBT or both.

11

Suicide Clusters and Contagion

Frank J. Zenere

Frank J. Zenere is the school psychologist for the Miami-Dade County Public School's Student Services Crisis Team in Florida. He is a past chairman of the National Association of School Psychologists National Emergency Assistance Team.

The dictionary defines "contagious" as "exciting similar emotions or conduct in others." The word can also apply to suicide; research has shown that a single suicide can increase suicidal behavior in others, and adolescents are especially vulnerable. Suicide contagion is more likely to occur among individuals who have witnessed a suicide, who have an emotional or social connection to the victim, or who have preexisting vulnerabilities, such as the presence of mental illness or a history of trauma exposure. School principals and faculty members can reduce the potential for suicide contagion by recognizing the warning signs, implementing screening programs to identify students at risk, and providing intervention and counseling services.

On Monday morning, Principal Edwards receives a telephone call from a distressed parent, informing him that her son Sam, a popular student athlete, died over the weekend. Before Edwards has the opportunity to offer his condolences, she whispers, "He killed himself." This is the second student death from the school in the past two months. In

Frank J. Zenere, "Suicide Clusters and Contagion," *Principal Leadership*, October 2009. Copyright © 2009 by National Association of Secondary School Principals. All rights reserved. Reproduced by permission.

March, a senior died of an overdose. Although not officially ruled a suicide, there is conjecture among the students that it was. Edwards calls the crisis team together to plan a response. The school psychologist, who also serves on the district crisis team, reports that there have been three additional suicides by students attending neighboring schools since Christmas break. One of those students played on the same travel soccer team as Sam. Is this a tragic coincidence or something more?

Suicide Postvention

Youth suicide is one of the most serious, preventable health problems in the United States. It is the third leading cause of death among adolescents. According to a recent national survey of students in grades 9–12, nearly 15% of respondents had seriously considered suicide and 7% actually had attempted suicide in the previous 12 months (Eaton et al., 2008). Moreover, suicide can be a contagious behavior that schools have the opportunity—and responsibility—to prevent.

Of primary concern following a youth suicide is the potential for contagion that can lead to cluster suicides.

Providing assistance in the aftermath of a youth suicide requires a delicate and well-planned approach; responding to the occurrence of multiple youth suicides provides an even greater challenge. The delivery of crisis response services in the aftermath of a youth suicide is referred to as *suicide postvention*, which is defined as "the provision of crisis intervention, support and assistance for those affected by a completed suicide." (American Association of Suicidology, 1998, p.1). The goals of postvention include supporting the survivors, preventing imitative suicides by identifying other individuals who are at risk for self-destructive behavior and connecting them to intervention services, reducing survivor identification with the deceased, and providing long-term surveillance and support (Gould & Kramer, 2001).

In addition, principals must help students and staff members stay focused on learning and maintaining a healthy school environment. School administrators will be in a better position both to provide this leadership and to support those who have been most affected by the loss when they understand the factors that drive suicide contagion and how to work with mental health staff members to identify students who are most at risk for secondary suicidal behavior.

Risk of Contagion

Of primary concern following a youth suicide is the potential for contagion that can lead to cluster suicides. Contagion is the process by which the suicidal behavior or a suicide influences an increase in the suicidal behaviors of others (U.S. Department of Health & Human Services, 2008). Multiple suicidal behaviors or suicides that occur within a defined geographical area and fall within an accelerated time frame may represent a potential cluster (Berman & Jobes, 1994). Research indicates that a single adolescent suicide increases the risk of additional suicides within a community and may serve as a catalyst for the development of a cluster (Gould, Wallenstein, & Kleinman, 1990; Gould, Wallenstein, Kleinman, O'Carroll, & Mercy, 1990).

Although suicide clusters are rare, they tend to be most prevalent among adolescents (Cavidson, 1989; Phillips & Carstensen, 1986), accounting for 1%–5% of teenage suicides and 100–200 deaths annually (Gould, n.d.). As part of her research, Gould (as cited in Joyce, 2008) identified 53 suicide clusters (defined as 3–11 victims, ranging from 13–20 years of age, who took their life within a one-year period) in the United States.

Identification of Contagion

Because adolescents are most at risk for contagion, the school community can play an important role in identifying students who are vulnerable to imitative suicide and intervene to decrease the propensity for lethal behavior. Some have argued that a single exposure to the suicidal behavior of another person does not result in imitative behavior but that exposure must be linked with a predisposed vulnerability factor to determine contagion (Berman & Jobes, 1994).

Youth may connect with a victim [of suicide] who has a similar life circumstance or view the deceased as a role model.

Suicide clusters have been viewed as the end result of a contagious disease in which vulnerable individuals connect to superinfect one another (Johansson, Lindqvist, & Eriksson, 2006). This perspective can be further detailed by examining a community trauma assessment model called "circles of vulnerability." This method, developed at the Community Stress Prevention Center in Kiryat Shmona, Israel, (Lahad & Cohen, 2006), can be used to determine the degree of emotional impact that a serious incident or disaster had on members of a community and to assess the impact of suicidal behavior or suicides on the greater community. It can also be used to identify individuals who are most at risk for said behavior. The model is best depicted as three intersecting circles that represent geographical proximity, psychosocial proximity, and population at risk.

Geographical proximity is the physical distance a person is from the location of an incident, including eye witnesses to a suicide or those discovering or exposed to the immediate aftermath of the event. Extensive and repetitive media coverage broadens this form of proximity by exposing more of the community to the potential deleterious effects associated with the death. Sensationalized coverage along with detailed information surrounding the event increases the likelihood of additional suicides (Gould, as cited in Joyce, 2008).

Psychological proximity is related to the level of identification an individual has to a victim. Examples include cultural or subcultural connections (Hendin, as cited in Berman & Jobes, 1994), victims of bullying, team members, classmates, those attending the same school, and others who perceive a unifying characteristic. Youth may connect with a victim who has a similar life circumstance or view the deceased as a role model. This phenomenon has been observed following the suicide of a perceived leader, a popular student, an athlete, or a celebrity, among others.

Social proximity refers to the relationship one has with the injured or deceased. Examples include family members, friends, romantic interests, acquaintances, or others who are part of the same social circle. Suicidal acts by someone close can provide a model for similar behavior. In her research, Gould (as cited in Joyce, 2008) found that victims of cluster suicides tend to know previous victims but are generally not best friends.

Population at risk encompasses those individuals who have been exposed to a traumatic event and who have one or more preexisting vulnerabilities that may influence the psychological and emotional impact of the current incident, including the presence of mental illness, a history of trauma exposure, prior suicidal behavior, substance abuse, and family conflict. Those factors create a foundation of instability that may lead an individual to consider suicide as a viable option.

Individuals who are at the greatest risk for contagion include those who witnessed the suicide or its immediate aftermath (geographical proximity), had a psychological or social connection to the deceased (psychosocial proximity), and have preexisting vulnerabilities (population at risk). Additional factors that enhance an individual's potential for contagion include facilitation of the suicide through supportive actions, failure to identify signs of suicidal intent, a feeling of responsibility for the death, a sense of helplessness or hopelessness, recent significant stress or loss, and limited social support (American Association of Suicidology, 1998; Davidson, 1989; Brock, 2002).

Cluster suicides are not the same phenomenon as suicide pacts or Internet suicides in which individuals commit to die together or at approximately the same time. Suicide pacts are uncommon among adolescents and are most often engaged in by the elderly or romantically involved individuals. Internet suicide is a relatively new phenomenon among adolescents and young adults, primarily in Japan, who do not know one another but connect over the Internet. Although cluster suicide victims share some connection, however fragile or self-perceived, they typically have not planned their deaths together.

Avoiding Contagion

Successful suicide postvention is dependent upon a timely, efficient, and targeted response to a student suicide. Principals must work seamlessly with faculty members, school mental health professionals, and support staff members to reduce the potential for contagion. This capacity is greatly enhanced when schools have ongoing suicide prevention programs and crisis teams that are trained to identify students at risk and provide appropriate supports, such as counseling and referrals. In fact, effective postvention is itself a primary form of prevention as well as support.

At the school level, the response to a student should include the following.

Confirm the facts. Verify that the death was by suicide, preferably by talking directly to the student's parents or an official source. Do not speculate. Visit the family of the deceased student to offer support.

Mobilize a crisis response team. Work with the team to inform faculty and staff members and to plan communications with students and families. Give staff members and parents information about risk factors and warning signs for suicidal behavior.

Identify at-risk students. Connect with students who may present an elevated risk for suicidal behavior. Notify their parents personally of the suicide and the possible increased risk to their children. Make referrals for community-based mental health services for parents and guardians of suicidal students.

Inform students through personal communications. Visit each of the victim's classes to tell students about the loss and give them facts. Equip teachers in other classes with talking points and access to a mental health professional to help manage student reactions. Avoid providing unnecessary details about the suicide. Never notify students in a large assembly or by a schoolwide announcement. When visiting the victim's classes:

- Tell students that prevention is key and inform them of the warning signs

- Convey that the victim is responsible for his or her actions

- Inform the students that suicide is often evidence of mental illness (potentially including substance abuse)

- Stress alternatives to suicide

- Normalize the emotions experienced by survivors

- Let students know that help is available

- Identify resources that students may use.

Support and monitor affected students. Give students opportunities to receive individual or small group counseling. Monitor student absences in the days following a suicide. Be open and accessible and emphasize that adults are there to help if students or their friends are struggling for any reason. Encourage parents to accompany their children if they plan to attend a community-based memorial service or funeral. Pro-. vide long-term surveillance of students who have been affected by the suicide.

Provide appropriate outlets for grieving. Develop living memorials that will help students cope with emotions and problems—for example, display appropriate prevention-related informational resources in the school's media center, make donations to a local crisis center, participate in an event that raises suicide prevention awareness, or create or expand a school counseling program. Include the victim's friends and family when making decisions about memorials. Do not create permanent memorials or dedications or hold a service on campus.

Engage the community. Suicide is a tragedy of the broader community as well as the school. Communication with other schools in the district or geographic area (including feeder schools) and groups with whom the student was involved (e.g., clubs, sports teams, jobs, and religious organizations) can help support survivors and identify potential contagion.

Perhaps the most important fact about suicide is that it is preventable in most cases.

When Contagion Is Suspected

The presence or increase of suicidal behavior (e.g., thoughts, threats, and attempts) among students after a single suicide may signal the beginning of the contagion process. Should this occur, immediate steps are required to contain the spread of self-destructive behavior before contagion takes hold. This can best be accomplished by seeking the support of the school psychologist or other school mental health professionals who can:

- Identify and assess students who are at risk for suicide

- Notify parents and guardians of the risk behaviors

- Recommend community-based mental health services to parents and guardians

- Train faculty members, parents, and students on how to recognize warning signs and identify support services

- Coordinate with local schools and community providers

- Consult with administrators, faculty members, and parents

- Help create a school climate that fosters positive connections among students and between students and adults.

The successful identification and containment of an active contagion may require a multidisciplinary, communitywide approach. Such stakeholders as school officials, law enforcement officers, emergency room directors, funeral directors, clergy, public health administrators, and representatives from mental health agencies can work collaboratively to develop a process and take appropriate actions to address a problem. Each group may have information that is valuable in making such determinations. Similar efforts have proven effective in halting suicide clusters in communities across the nation.

Reaffirm Prevention Efforts

Perhaps the most important fact about suicide is that it is preventable in most cases. Schools are essential to prevention efforts because they know and have access to students and their families on a regular basis. They have the facility to teach students and staff members the signs and symptoms of depression and suicide and to implement universal screening programs, such as Columbia TeenScreen and the SOS Signs of Suicide Program, to help identify students at risk. Effective prevention should be integrated into comprehensive school mental health services through which school-based professionals provide training, crisis response, intervention, counseling, and referrals to community services. Ongoing prevention not only helps save lives but also greatly enhances schools' ability to respond effectively when tragedy does occur.

Conclusion

The suicide of a student is one of the most difficult crises faced by a principal. It bears both the terrible loss of any untimely death of a young person and the increased psychological risks to others in the school community. Principals play a pivotal role in the early recognition of indicators that may promote the process of contagion. Preparation and collaboration with school mental health and crisis personnel to implement timely and effective postvention practices can disrupt, if not extinguish, contagion.

References

- American Association of Suicidology. (1998). Suicide postvention guidelines: Suggestions for dealing with the aftermath of suicide in schools. Washington, DC: Author.

- Berman, A.L., & Jobes, D.A. (1994). Adolescent suicide assessment and intervention. Washington, DC: American Psychological Association.

- Brock, S.E. (2002). School suicide postvention. In S.E. Brock, P.J. Lazarus, & S.R. Jimerson (Eds.), Best practices in school crisis prevention and intervention (pp. 553–576). Bethesda, MD: National Association of School Psychologists.

- Davidson, L.E. (1989). Suicide cluster and youth. In C.R. Pfeffer (Ed.), Suicide among youth (pp. 83–99). Washington, DC: American Psychiatric Press.

- Eaton, D.K., Kann, L., Kinchen, S., Shanklin, S., Ross, J., Hawkins, J., et al. (2008). Youth risk behavior surveillance@mdash;United States, 2007. Retrieved February 14, 2009, from www.cdc.gov/mmwr/preview/mmwrhtml/ss5704a1.htm

- Gould, M.S. (n.d.). Suicide contagion (clusters). Retrieved October 13, 2008, from http://suicideandmentalhealthassociationinternational.org/suiconclust.html

- Gould, M.S., & Kramer, R.A. (2001). Youth suicide prevention. Suicide and Life-Threatening Behavior, 31, 6–31.

- Gould, M.S., Wallenstein, S., & Kleinman, M.H. (1990). Time-space clustering of teenage suicide. American Journal of Epidemiology, 131, 71–78.

- Gould, M.S., Walleinstein, S., Kleinman, M.H., O'Carroll, P., & Mercy, J. (1990). Suicide clusters: An examination of agespecific effects, American Journal of Public Health, 80, 211–212.

- Johansson, L., Lindqvist, P., & Eriksson, A. (2006). Teenage suicide cluster formation and contagion: Implications for primary care. BMC Family Practice, 7. Retrieved from www.biomedcentral.com/1471-2296/7/32

- Joyce, J. (2008). Unraveling the suicide clusters. In BBC News. Retrieved October 13, 2008, from http://news.bbc.co.uk/go/em/fr/-/2/hi/uk_news/7205141.stm

- Lahad, M., & Cohen, A. (2006). The community stress prevention center: 25 years of community stress prevention and intervention. Kiryat Shmona, Israel: The Community Stress Prevention Center.

- Phillips, D.P., & Carstensen, L.L.(1986). Clustering of teenage suicides after television news stories about suicide. New England Journal of Medicine, 315, 685–698.

- U.S. Department of Health & Human Services. (2008). What does "suicide contagion" mean, and what can be done to prevent it? Retrieved October 13, 2008, from http://answers.hhs.gov/questions/3146

12

Internet Use Affects Teen Suicide Risk in Positive and Negative Ways

Tony Durkee et al.

Tony Durkee is associated with the Department of Learning, Informatics, Management, and Ethics at the National Centre for Suicide Research and Prevention of Mental Ill-Health, Karolinska Institute, in Stockholm, Sweden. His coauthors include Gergo Hadlaczky, Michael Westerlund, and Vladimir Carli. Both Hadlaczky and Carli also work at the National Centre for Suicide Research and Prevention of Mental Ill-Health, while Westerlund works in the Department of Journalism, Media, and Communication at the University of Stockholm.

Various studies have shown that Internet usage does have an effect on suicidal behavior, particularly among isolated and vulnerable adolescents. The results of the studies illustrate that pro-suicide websites and online discussion groups encourage suicide and suicide pacts, and can even bully individuals into committing suicide. On the other hand, the research also shows that the Internet can be an effective and positive tool for suicide prevention by providing stigmatized, reclusive, or other at-risk individuals a supportive and sympathetic network. This duality in which the Internet provides both positive and negative effects is referred to as the Internet Paradox.

Suicidal behaviour is a compelling public health issue, particularly among adolescents and young adults. . . .

External factors that may affect the relationship between suicidal behaviour and mental health should be taken into consideration during risk assessment and prevention efforts. Among those factors which have particular relevance today, is Internet use. The Internet can serve as a channel with positive and/or negative effects on users' psychological health and well-being. [A.O.] Alao *et al.* and [N.] D'Hulster and [C.] Van Heeringen shared this ambivalence, and suggested that the Internet can encourage suicidal behaviour by its supply of descriptions of suicide methods and pro-suicide websites, wherein individuals with severe mental health problems are advised not to seek help and, at the same time, if the Internet is used properly, it can also be a key resource for helping potentially suicidal individuals.

The Internet Paradox

Referred to as the Internet paradox, both positive and negative effects of Internet use are observed. Observed positive effects of the Internet include the ability to utilize and disseminate information quickly and accessibly. In this context, Internet use appears very effective in a number of areas such as providing health information, serving as a platform for education, social networks and support, entertainment, and even mental health promotion and prevention programs. The negative consequences of Internet use often coincide with social and risk-behavioural problems. Research shows that adolescents who are susceptible to social exclusion, bully victimization and substance abuse may utilize the Internet as a coping mechanism in an attempt to relieve stress. It is under such conditions that adolescents become the most vulnerable for incipient online risks, including cyber-bullying, pathological Internet use, pro-suicide websites, facilitation of suicide pacts, and expedition of suicide methods. As global Internet user rates are rising, the reliance on the Internet and ensuing on-line risks are increasing as well.

Internet use has grown exponentially worldwide, comprising now nearly two billion users. With regards to geographic distribution, in 2010 the largest number of Internet users was located within the Asian region, which accounted for 42% of global Internet users. Europe accounted for the second highest region, with 24.2%, followed by North America (13.5%), Latin America (10.4%), Africa (5.6%), Middle East (3.2%) and Oceania/Australia (1.1%). . . .

On pro-suicide websites, society and its institutions are seen as a threat to the individual's 'natural rights' to take their lives.

The increase in Internet usage is also illustrated predominantly among the adolescent age-groups. In EU-27 [European Union], statistics demonstrate that 90% of young people aged 16–24 years used the Internet regularly during 2010. Due to the widespread use of the Internet on most continents, research concerning its implications on mental health and suicidal behaviours necessitate scientific review.

The general aim of this study was to review the scientific literature concerning the Internet and suicidality; and examine the different pathways by which suicidal risks and prevention efforts are facilitated through the Internet. . . .

Some Websites Encourage Suicidal Behavior

The Internet provides an assortment of viable websites providing endless access to information. However, is the information persons are retrieving always correct, or even safe? At present, there are a large number of pro-suicide websites in several different languages on the Internet, and they often rank high on the search engines' results pages. These often interlinking websites feature similar characteristics in offering content, wherein suicidal acts are promoted, and typically utilized as a means for individuals to cope with problems in life. In some instances, while no motivation is given, taking one's life is encouraged as a form of rebellion against the prohibition of suicide. [K.] Becker and [M.H.] Schmidt have termed this aspect as a clear 'anti-psychiatric' view, which manifests itself through disseminating information on the most effective ways to commit suicide, as well as propagating that suicide should be reflected as an individual choice. On pro-suicide websites, society and its institutions are seen as a threat to the individual's 'natural rights' to take their lives. These messages reach a relatively large number of vulnerable persons, with social and psychological problems, as well as those who are actually seeking help on the Internet.

The existing studies on pro-suicide websites have mainly focused on the classification of website content. This is performed by entering keywords and phrases related to suicide into a search engine. Websites ranking highest in the search are scrutinized for suicidal content and profiled as pro-suicide, suicide-neutral or anti-suicide.

[L.] Biddle and colleagues conducted a study in which they examined various search engines, including Google, Yahoo!, MSN and ASK, and the outcomes each particular search engine displayed when entering select keyword and phrases, e.g., (a) suicide; (b) suicide methods; (c) suicide sure methods; (d) most effective methods of suicide, *etc.*. Subsequently, as users seldom look beyond the first ten hits on the results page, the study outcomes were thus confined to this criterion. This generated a total of 480 results. The study indicated that nearly 30% of the content of web pages was subjugated by material concerning suicide methods. Suicidal acts ranged from incitement, provocation to non-rejection. Conversely, 25% of the webpage content focused on suicide prevention, with a distinctive opposition to suicidal behaviours, while 40% were construed as embracing, to some extent, a position of suicide prevention.

[P.R.] Recupero and colleagues investigated the accessibility of harmful online resources for suicidal persons. The authors utilized five popular search engines: Google, Yahoo!, ASK, Lycos and Dogpile. The authors entered four suicide-related search terms: (a) suicide; (b) how to commit suicide; (c) suicide methods; and (d) how to kill yourself. Search outcomes were categorized as *pro-suicide, anti-suicide, suicide-neutral, not a suicide site,* or *error (i.e.,* page would not load). Results showed 373 web pages comprising suicidal content. Among those web pages, 11% was considered to contain obvious pro-suicide material; 30% was deemed to be suicide-neutral, and 29% was anti-suicide.

Participants exhort one another to follow through with their suicidal plans.

It is important to note that pro-suicide communication on the Internet seems to have become more common over time. A study using the Google search engine to investigate the prevalence of suicide-related material on the Internet showed that there was a proportional increase in pro-suicide messages and discussions between 2005 and 2009. . . .

Pro-suicide websites are produced in opposition to socially dominant attitudes on the topic of suicide. In our society, the issue remains to question the primacy or sanctity of life. To advocate the individual's 'right' to end their life is the primary argument from the pro-suicide view. It is an effective weapon in the struggle against society's established morals and values. Descriptions of suicide on pro-suicide websites are, thus, tools for distinguishing the self and the group from the worldview of the dominant culture. Although construction of the pro-suicide approach can, in many ways, reflect a destructive ac-

tivity, it also constitutes a meaningful activity for its protago-
nists. The reasons why pro-suicide content is produced and
available for public access is perhaps conceived as a meaningful identity-constructive role it fulfils for the producers.

[D.] Baker and [S.] Fortune argued that discussions in
various studies and media have been too generalized, lacking
in-depth knowledge concerning Internet communication on
suicide and self-harm, and its insinuation for those involved.
Based on ten in-depth interviews, with people who regularly
visited self-injury and suicide forums, the authors concluded
that these forums provided participants a source of empathy,
fellowship and coping with social and psychological problems.

---

*Suicide pacts often develop in chat rooms or on message
boards, which endorse suicidal behaviours.*

[M.] Westerlund noted that visitors on interactive suicide
forums are provided with an opportunity to discuss difficult
experiences, which would not be possible in most other con-
texts. Participants are not held accountable to institutional fig-
ures or regulations. Their discussions, however, can potentially
be destructive, wherein information concerning potent suicide
methods are discussed and exchanged, and participants exhort
one another to follow through with their suicidal plans. The
atmosphere can also be aggressive, with elements of verbal in-
sults and bullying, possibly having a negative impact on individuals who already feel exposed and vulnerable. At the same
time, a comforting, supportive and understanding attitude can
be found in many exchanges. There is an opportunity to meet
other people who share similar experiences, wherein their
thoughts and feelings are not condemned nor lectured about.
Supportive and consoling discussions, composed with aggressive and destructive elements, become a flow of poly-
phonic voices. In view of this ambiguity, it is important to

take a balanced view and avoid focusing solely on the potential risks inherent in chat rooms such as these.

Notwithstanding, pro-suicide websites are detrimental among a subgroup of persons with mental health problems, especially if the person is susceptible to social isolation and lacks a social network to counterbalance the negative information they may receive from such harmful websites. Pro-suicide websites often provide an open forum to discuss methods and plans for committing the suicidal act itself. Under these types of settings and circumstances is where suicidal pacts can emerge.

Suicide Pacts on the Internet

The definition of a suicide pact is a cooperative choice by two or more individuals who agree that both, or all, will commit suicide together, in a prearranged place and at a designated time. Research concerning the Internet and suicidal behaviour, in this aspect, investigates what is known as "net suicides", *i.e.*, suicide pacts made on the Internet.

Evidence shows that suicide pacts often develop in chat rooms or on message boards, which endorse suicidal behaviours. This milieu attracts vulnerable persons feeling socially excluded from society. The socially-isolated individual can communicate interactively and anonymously, thus, exposing him/herself to impending pro-suicidal incitement from one or more parties involved. This could potentially lead to the coordination of a suicide pact.

An example of such a tragedy occurred in Japan during 2004 when nine people took their own lives, in a suicide pact, initiated and coordinated over the Internet. According to [A.] Naito, in Japan alone some 60 persons a year are presumed to have died from 'net suicides' and these trends appear to be on the increase. However, this occurrence is not only limited to

Japan. Online suicide pacts have been reported in other nations as well, including the United Kingdom, Norway and South Korea.

The Internet can prove invaluable in reaching those individuals, who otherwise are unattainable, in order to promote mental health and prevent suicidal behaviours.

Destructive communication through Internet websites has augmented the suicidal risks for vulnerable individuals. In some cases, persons are coerced into consenting to a suicide pact by unknown accomplices. In other cases, acquaintances or friends decide collectively to formulate a suicide pact. Notwithstanding, this phenomenon may explicate the spread of new suicide methods across continents. In Japan, during 2008, there was a sudden increase in hydrogen sulphide poisoning, which developed as a potential method for committing suicide. This was eventually linked to a website that disseminated material on a new technique for manufacturing gas, which was then transmitted through message boards on the Internet. As the trend rapidly spread through Internet communication, the new suicide method began emerging in other parts of the world.

In contrast to the potential risks of cyber technology, there is a clear advantage to having the ability to quickly access information and to interactively communicate with individuals in real-time, while maintaining anonymity. This Internet pathway has significant potential for promoting prevention efforts and reaching vulnerable risk-groups.

Suicide Prevention via the Internet

The prevention of suicide and suicidal behaviour is an important public health concern, yet, the topic of suicide is still subjected to stigmatization. Suicidal behaviour has shown to significantly correlate with multiple psychopathologies, such as:

depression, schizophrenia, anxiety, impulsivity, social phobias, obsessive-compulsive and affective disorders. Adolescents and young people often share comorbid risk-factors associated with suicidality, which are not always a diagnosable disorder, rather are often presented through risk-taking behaviours. There is substantial evidence showing a strong correlation between suicidality and different forms of risk-behaviours, including: NSSI [non-suicidal self injury], substance abuse, tobacco use, delinquency, aggression, bullying, and promiscuous sexual behaviour. These groups are the most susceptible for incipient suicidal behaviours. Therefore, this group would be the ones who would probably benefit the most from receiving anonymous treatment online, wherein they can openly discuss their feelings without being exposed to the stigmatization and taboo of discussing mental health issues and suicidality. The ability to remain anonymous in a conversational community increases the willingness to confess and discuss thoughts and feelings related to suicide, mental pain and vulnerability, while reducing the risk of self-censorship. Given the uniqueness of this specific risk-group, the Internet can prove invaluable in reaching those individuals, who otherwise are unattainable, in order to promote mental health and prevent suicidal behaviours.

Effective prevention strategies targeting this particular risk-group should include components that increase awareness and help-seeking behaviours, while decreasing risk-taking and suicidal behaviours, thereby, reducing stigma. [D.] Wasserman and [T.] Durkee have delineated specific approaches often utilized in suicide preventive interventions, among which, includes the Universal/Selective/Indicated (USI) model. In the USI model, the universal intervention targets the general population, the selective intervention targets subgroups at-risk for suicide, and the indicated intervention is aimed at high-risk suicidal individuals who already have begun self-destructive behaviours. The USI model that adopts the conceptual framework of increasing awareness, education and de-stigmatizing mechanisms would be a theoretical basis in developing an effective Internet-based prevention program.

Literature suggests that web-based communication can provide support to suicidal individuals. In one study, performed over a 11-month period, the results illustrated that the discussion members on a website, converging on the theme of suicide, provided a supportive network, based on shared experiences, sympathy, acceptance and encouragement.

In another study, a web-based intervention on treatment-seeking among college students at-risk for suicidality was examined. Participants from two universities were invited to complete an online survey that screened for depression and other suicidal risk-factors. Respondents received a modified and personal assessment and were able to converse anonymously with an online clinical therapist. Students classified as at-risk were advised to appear in-person for evaluation and treatment. Results yielded 1162 students, in which 8% of invitees completed the screening questionnaire; 981 (84.4%) were considered to be at high or moderate risk. Among this cluster, 190 (19.4%) joined a personal examination session, and 132 (13.5%) entered therapy. Outcomes stipulated that students who engaged in online discussions, with the clinical therapist, were three-times more likely than the in-person attendees to come for evaluation and enter treatment.

Organizations to Contact

The editors have compiled the following list of organizations concerned with the issues debated in this book. The descriptions are derived from materials provided by the organizations. All have publications or information available for interested readers. The list was compiled on the date of publication of the present volume; names, addresses, phone and fax numbers, and e-mail and Internet addresses may change. Be aware that many organizations take several weeks or longer to respond to inquiries, so allow as much time as possible.

American Association of Suicidology (AAS)
5221 Wisconsin Ave. NW, Washington, DC   20015
(202) 237-2280 • fax: (202) 237-2282
website: www.suicidology.org

The American Association of Suicidology is one of the largest suicide prevention organizations in the United States. It promotes the view that suicidal thoughts are almost always a symptom of depression and that suicide is almost never a rational decision. In addition to suicide prevention, AAS also works to increase public awareness about suicide and to help those grieving the loss of a loved one to suicide. The association publishes the quarterly newsletters *Surviving Suicide* and *Newslink,* and the journal *Suicide and Life Threatening Behavior.*

American Foundation for Suicide Prevention (AFSP)
120 Wall St., 29th Floor, New York, NY   10005
(888) 333-2377 • fax: (212) 363-6237
e-mail: inquiry@afsp.org
website: www.afsp.org

Formerly known as the American Suicide Foundation, AFSP supports scientific research on depression and suicide, educates the public and professionals on the recognition and treatment of depressed and suicidal individuals, and provides support programs for those coping with the loss of a loved one to suicide. AFSP publishes informational handouts and brochures, including *Surviving After Suicide Brochure* and *When You Fear Someone May Take Their Life Brochure.*

American Psychiatric Association (APA)
1000 Wilson Blvd., Suite 1825, Arlington, VA   22209-3901
(703) 907-7300
e-mail: apa@psych.org
website: www.psych.org

An organization of psychiatrists dedicated to studying the nature, treatment, and prevention of mental disorders, the American Psychiatric Association helps create mental health policies, distributes information about psychiatry, and promotes psychiatric research and education. It publishes the *American Journal of Psychiatry* and *Psychiatric News* monthly.

American Psychological Association (APA)
750 First St. NE, Washington, DC   20002-4242
(800) 374-2721
website: www.apa.org

The American Psychological Association aims to "advance the creation, communication, and application of psychological knowledge to benefit society and improve people's lives." It produces numerous publications, including the book *The Adolescent Brain*, the brochures *Suicide Warning Signs* and *Resilience for Teens: Got Bounce*, and the newsletter *In the Public Interest.*

Brain Injury Association of America (BIAA)
1608 Spring Hill Rd., Suite 110, Vienna, VA   22182
(703) 761-0750 • fax: (703) 761-0755
website: www.biausa.org

The nation's oldest and largest brain injury organization, the Brain Injury Association of America offers education, research, and advocacy for individuals with brain injury, their families and friends, and healthcare professionals. BIAA consists of a nationwide network of more than forty chartered state affiliates and hundreds of local chapters and support groups. Its National Directory of Brain Injury Services offers a comprehensive online directory of traumatic brain injury providers. The organization publishes fact sheets and the quarterly magazine, *THE Challenge!*.

Canadian Association for Suicide Prevention (CASP)

870 Portage Ave., Winnipeg, MB   R3G0P1
  Canada
(204) 784-4073
e-mail: casp@casp-acps.ca
website: www.suicideprevention.ca

CASP organizes annual conferences and educational programs on suicide prevention. Among its publications are *E-Bulletins*, the newsletter *CASP News*, and the article "Suicide Grief."

Centre for Suicide Prevention (CSP)

Suite 320, 105 12 Ave. SE, Calgary, AB   T2G 1A1
  Canada
(403) 245-3900 • fax: (403) 245-0299
website: http://suicideinfo.ca

Originally created in 1981 as the Suicide Information and Education Centre (SIEC), the organization's primary mandate was to create a specialized library on the issue of suicide. In 2005, SIEC incorporated under a new name: Centre for Suicide Prevention. Believing that prevention is the only solution to suicide, CSP is an education center designed to equip individuals and organizations with the information, knowledge, and skills necessary to respond to the risk of suicide. The center publishes the *Suicide Awareness Brochure* and the *Suicide Help Card*, as well as the booklets *Cyber Bullying* and the *Suicide Intervention Handbook*.

Depression and Bipolar Support Alliance (DBSA)
730 N Franklin St., Suite 501, Chicago, IL   60654-7225
(800) 826-3632 • fax: (312) 642-7243
website: www.dbsalliance.org

The Depression and Bipolar Support Alliance provides support, education, and advocacy for patients with depression and bipolar disorder. It offers those living with mental illness the opportunity to participate in peer-based, recovery-centered, and empowerment-focused treatment options. It publishes the monthly DBSA eUpdate newsletter and various books and brochures, including *Myths and Facts about Depression and Bipolar Disorder* and *Coping with Unexpected Events: Depression and Trauma*.

Harvard School of Public Health (HSPH)
677 Huntington Ave., Boston, MA   02115
website: www.hsph.harvard.edu

The mission of the Harvard School of Public Health is to prevent disease and advance the public's health through research, higher education, and communication. HSPH publishes a monthly *HSPH Update* newsletter, a monthly *Nutrition Update* newsletter, and *The Kiosk: HSPH E-News and Notices*, as well as a number of articles concerning the issue of suicide.

International Foundation for Research and Education on Depression (iFred)
PO Box 17598, Baltimore, MD   21297-1598
(410) 268-0044 • fax: (443) 782-0739
e-mail: info@ifred.org
website: www.ifred.org

The International Foundation for Research and Education on Depression is one of the few organizations concerned with researching the causes of depression and helping those coping with depression on an international scale. Through education and destigmatization efforts, iFred promotes both the general recognition that depression co-occurs with other illnesses, and the worldwide conviction that depression can be effectively and sensitively treated. It has produced flyers outlining the effects of depression on both individuals and businesses, and has launched the Field of Hope campaign aimed at illustrating the frequency with which depression is diagnosed, and the Project Honor campaign aimed at helping returning soldiers cope with depression and successfully transition to civilian life. Its website also offers a blog and a depression self-assessment test.

Jason Foundation

18 Volunteer Dr., Hendersonville, TN   37075
website: www.jasonfoundation.com

The Jason Foundation is dedicated to educating students, teachers, and community organizations about the risk and prevention of teen suicide. It operates a crisis hotline aimed at assisting individuals in need of immediate help and creates multimedia resource packages designed for larger educational efforts. The Jason Foundation publishes several educational brochures and produces the "A Promise for Tomorrow" education curriculum, which promotes teen suicide awareness and prevention among seventh through twelfth graders.

Jed Foundation

1140 Broadway, Suite 803, New York, NY   10001
(212) 647-7544 • fax: (212) 647-7542
e-mail: support@jedfoundation.org
website: www.jedfoundation.org

The Jed Foundation is a charitable organization concerned with reducing suicide among US college and university students. Established in 2000 by two parents mourning the suicide death of their twenty-year-old son, it raises awareness of suicide deaths on college campuses and forges connections between academic communities researching teen suicide and higher education professionals directly connected with college-aged students. The Jed Foundation developed Ulifeline, an Internet-based resource for students struggling with depression and stress, and has developed multiple educational programs aimed at campus-wide education and prevention. The organization also publishes a newsletter.

National Alliance on Mental Illness (NAMI)
3803 N Fairfax Dr., Suite 100, Arlington, VA   22203
(703) 524-7600 • fax: (703) 524-9094
website: www.nami.org

NAMI is a consumer advocacy and support organization composed largely of family members of people with severe mental illnesses such as schizophrenia, bipolar disorder, and depression. The alliance adheres to the position that severe mental illnesses are biological brain diseases and that mentally ill people should not be blamed or stigmatized for their conditions. NAMI favors increased government funding for research, treatment, and community services for the mentally ill. Its publications include the magazine *NAMI Advocate*, the quarterly magazine *NAMI Beginnings*, as well as various brochures, handbooks, and policy recommendations. Its website also operates the NAMI Blog.

Samaritans
PO Box 9090, Stirling   FK8 2SA
  UK
+44 (0) 8457 909090
e-mail: jo@samaritans.org
website: www.samaritans.org.uk

Samaritans is the largest suicide prevention organization in the world. Established in England in 1953, the organization now has branches in at least forty-four nations throughout the world. The group's volunteers provide confidential counseling and other assistance to suicidal and despondent individuals. Samaritans publishes a monthly newsletter and the *Information Resource Pack*.

Society for the Prevention of Teen Suicide (SPTS)
110 W Main St., Freehold, NJ   07728

e-mail: info@sptsnj.org
website: www.sptsusa.org

Founded in 2005 by Scott Fritz and Don Quigley, two friends who lost teenaged children to suicide, the Society for the Prevention of Teen Suicide's mission is to reduce the number of youth suicides and attempted suicides by encouraging overall public awareness through the development and promotion of educational training programs for teens, parents, and educators. SPTS publishes many resources, including *When a Friend Dies: Guidelines for Students, When a Friend Is Talking About Suicide,* and for parents, *Talking to Your Kids About Suicide.* The website also offers educators a two-hour suicide awareness training program and other training materials.

Suicide Awareness Voices of Education (SAVE)
8120 Penn Ave. S, Suite 470, Bloomington, MN   55431
(952) 946-7998
e-mail: save@save.org
website: www.save.org

SAVE works to prevent suicide and to help those grieving after the suicide of a loved one. Its members believe that brain diseases, such as depression, should be detected and treated promptly because they can result in suicide. In addition to pamphlets and the book *Suicide Survivors: A Guide for Those Left Behind,* the organization publishes the quarterly newsletter *Voices of Save* and the booklets *A Suicide Prevention Guide for Young People: What to Do, Parents as Partners,* and *Suicide: Coping with the Loss of a Friend or Loved One.*

Youth Suicide Prevention Program (YSPP)
444 NE Ravenna Blvd., Suite 103, Seattle, WA   98115
(206) 297-5922 • fax: (206) 297-0818
e-mail: info@yspp.org
website: www.yspp.org

The Youth Suicide Prevention Program is firmly dedicated to reducing the number of teen suicides mourned each year. Focusing on public awareness, training, and community action, it prioritizes awareness and education. YSPP publishes a newsletter and a blog, as well as *A Parent's Guide to Recognizing and Treating Depression in Your Child* and the brochure *Watch for Signs—Stop Youth Suicide.*

Bibliography

Books

David A. Brent, Kimberly D. Poling, and Tina R. Goldstein — *Treating Depressed and Suicidal Adolescents.* New York: Guilford Press, 2011.

Linda Carroll and David Rosner — *The Concussion Crisis: Anatomy of a Silent Epidemic.* New York: Simon & Schuster, 2011.

Katy Sara Culling — *Screaming in Silence: Suicide, Attempted Suicide and Self-Harm Recovery.* Essex, United Kingdom: Chipmunka Publishing, 2010.

Nick Dubin — *Asperger Syndrome: A Guide to Successful Stress Management.* Philadelphia, PA: Jessica Kingsley Publishers, 2009.

Ian H. Gotlib and Constance L. Hammen, eds. — *Handbook of Depression,* 2nd ed. New York: Guilford Press, 2009.

Thomas Joiner — *Why People Die by Suicide.* Cambridge, MA: Harvard University Press, 2007.

Thomas Joiner — *Myths About Suicide.* Cambridge, MA: Harvard University Press, 2011.

Gerald A. Juhnke, Paul F. Granello, and Darcy Haag Granello — *Suicide and Violence in the Schools: Assessment, Prevention, and Intervention Strategies.* Hoboken, NJ: John Wiley & Sons, 2011.

Mary Ann Keatley and Laura L. Whittemore — *Understanding Mild Traumatic Brain Injury (MTBI): An Insightful Guide to Symptoms, Treatments, and Redefining Recovery.* Boulder, CO: Brain Injury Hope Foundation, 2010.

Angerona S. Love — *When Darkness Comes: Saying "No" to Suicide.* Brookfield, CT: Insight Solutions, 2010.

Christopher Lukas and Henry Seiden — *Silent Grief: Living in the Wake of Suicide.* Philadelphia, PA: Jessica Kingsley Publishers, 2007.

Eric Marcus — *Why Suicide? Questions and Answers About Suicide, Suicide Prevention, and Coping with the Suicide of Someone You Know.* New York: Harper One, 2010.

Michael A. McCrea — *Mild Traumatic Brain Injury and Postconcussion Syndrome.* New York: Oxford University Press, 2007.

William P. Meehan — *Kids, Sports, and Concussion: A Guide for Coaches and Parents.* Santa Barbara, CA: Praeger, 2011.

David N. Miller — *Child and Adolescent Suicidal Behavior: School-Based Prevention, Assessment, and Intervention.* New York: Guilford Press, 2010.

Christopher Nowinski — *Head Games: Football's Concussion Crisis from the NFL to Youth Leagues.* Plymouth, MA: Drummond Publishing Group, 2006.

Dan Savage and Terry Miller, eds.	*It Gets Better: Coming Out, Overcoming Bullying, and Creating a Life Worth Living.* New York: Dutton Books, 2011.
Leo Sher and Alexander Vilens	*Internet and Suicide.* Hauppauge, NY: Nova Science Publishers, 2009.
Sarah Smyth	*The Other Side of Mind: A Journey through Bipolar Disorder.* Bloomington, IN: iUniverse, 2010.
Dana Worchel and Robin E. Gearing	*Suicide, Assessment and Treatment: Empirical and Evidence-Based Practices.* New York: Springer Publishing, 2010.

Periodicals and Internet Sources

Arthur Allen	"Listening to the Black Box: Did the FDA's Warnings on Antidepressants Have Any Effect on Teen Suicide?" *Slate*, September 15, 2009. www.slate .com.
Scott Anderson	"The Urge to End It All," *New York Times Magazine*, July 6, 2008.
Associated Press	"Girls' Suicide Rates Rise Dramatically," CBS News, February 11, 2009. www.cbsnews.com.
Kaitlin Bell Barnett	"Boy Interrupted: Bipolar Depression and a Teen's Suicide—Where Did Medication Fit In?" PsychCentral, January 28, 2012. http://blogs.psych central.com.

Emily Bazelon   "The Problem with *Bully*: The New
                       Documentary Dangerously
                       Oversimplifies the Connection
                       Between Bullying and Suicide," *Slate*,
                       March 29, 2012. www.slate.com.

Sara Blumberg   "Tale of Bullying at Arundel High,"
                       CapitalGazette.com, March 18, 2012.
                       www.capitalgazette.com.

Brendan Borrell   "Pros and Cons of Screening Teens
                       for Depression," *Los Angeles Times*,
                       August 3, 2009.

Dana Goldstein   "On Bullying, Teen Suicide, and the
                       Rush to Ascribe Blame (Often to
                       Schools)," DanaGoldstein.net, April 3,
                       2012. www.danagoldstein.net.

Jesse Green   "The Leap," *New York Magazine*, May
                       30, 2010.

Tara Haelle   "Teen Athletes Aren't Always
                       Hard-Headed: Concussions from
                       Sports Appear to Cause Greater
                       Damage in Teens than in Adults or
                       Children," DailyRx, February 28,
                       2012. www.dailyrx.com.

Mark L.   "The Social Environment and Suicide
Hatzenbuehler   Attempts in Lesbian, Gay, and
                       Bisexual Youth," *Pediatrics*, vol. 127,
                       no. 5, pp. 896–903, April 18, 2011.

Angela Haupt   "Health Buzz: Support Helps Prevent
                       Suicide Among Gay Youth," *U.S.
                       News & World Report*, April 18, 2011.

Martha L.
Hernandez

"Teen's Suicide Highlights Importance of Education Prevention," *The Monitor*, February 12, 2012.

Courtney
Hutchison

"Family Support for Gay Teens Saves Lives," ABCNews, December 6, 2010. http://abcnews.go.com.

Indian Health
Service

"American Indian/Alaska Native National Suicide Prevention Strategic Plan," August 2011. www.ihs.gov.

John Keilman

"Teen Suicide: More Schools Bring Issue Out of Shadows," *Chicago Tribune*, February 21, 2011.

Deanna LaMotte

"Gun Safety Will Prevent Suicides," *Chapel Hill News*, January 29, 2012.

Nestor
Lopez-Duran

"Antidepressant Medications and Risk for Suicide in Children and Adolescents: All Drugs Are Created Equal," Child-Psych, May 12, 2010. www.child-psych.org.

John Merrow

"Preventing Teen Suicide," *Huffington Post*, November 2, 2010. www.huffingtonpost.com.

Kenneth Miller

"Gay Teens Bullied to the Point of Suicide," *Ladies' Home Journal*, November 2010.

Benjamin Radford

"Is There a Gay Teen Suicide Epidemic?" LiveScience, October 8, 2010. www.livescience.com.

Lynne Soraya | "The Pain of Isolation: Asperger's and Suicide," *Psychology Today*, November 17, 2010.

Alix Spiegel | "A Fresh Look at Antidepressants Finds Low Risk of Youth Suicide," National Public Radio, February 7, 2012. www.npr.org.

Michael Stratford | "Preventing Suicide May Mean Fences and Nets, Not Just Counseling," *The Chronicle of Higher Education*, vol. 58, no. 30, March 25, 2012.

Jay Tavare | "Life or Death: Teen Suicide on American Indian Reservations," *Huffington Post*, February 12, 2011. www.huffingtonpost.com.

Allie Tempus | "A Tribal Tragedy: High Native American Suicide Rates Persist," WisconsinWatch.org, November 21, 2010. www.wisconsinwatch.org.

Lorna Thackeray | "Reasons for Suicide Amplified for Native Americans," *The Billings Gazette*, February 20, 2011.

Michelle Trudeau | "Media Should Tread Carefully in Covering Suicide," National Public Radio, November 30, 2009. www.npr.org.

Joseph White | "Parents Seek Answers for Son's Concussion, Suicide," *Sporting News*, August 30, 2011. www.sportingnews.com.

Jeff Yalden   "3 Reasons Why Teens Attempt
                Suicide," JeffYaldenBlog, February 12,
                2012. www.jeffyaldenblog.com.

Index

A

Absenteeism from bullying, 28
Acculturation stress, 14
Adult suicide, 21–22
African-American youth, 11
Agatston, Patti, 29
Aggression, 15, 27, 94, 97
Alao, A. O., 90
Alcohol use/abuse, 16, 48–49
American College of Obstetricians and Gynecologists, 7
American Foundation for Suicide Prevention, 34, 35
American Indian/Alaska Native (AI/AN) youth suicides
  community and cultural traditions, 49–50
  cumulative trauma over, 47–49
  overview, 40–41, 46–47
  programs against, 46–52
  rates of, 41–43, 47–48
  risk of, 11, 40–45, 41
  vulnerability to, 43–45
American Indian Campus Suicide Prevention Program, 50
American Journal of Public Health, 58
American Psychiatric Association, 7
American Psychological Association, 41, 45
Anti-bullying advocates, 34
Antidepressants
  concept behind, 71–72
  knowledge about, 72–74

research on, 74–76
suicidality risks, 73
suicide link, 14, 36
suicide prevention, 70–76
Anxiety
  Asperger's syndrome and, 64
  from bullying, 34
  suicidal intent, 12, 97
Asian-American/Pacific Islander youth, 11
Asperger, Hans, 62
Asperger's syndrome
  characteristics of, 62–64
  communication skills, 65–68
  depression and, 64–65
  feelings of teens with, 64
  managing emotions, 68–69
  overview, 24, 30, 61–62
  as suicide risk, 61–69
Attwood, Tony, 61–69

B

Baker, D., 94
Barrasso, John, 40–41
Bazelon, Emily, 36
Becker, K., 92
Bernik, Lidia, 35
Biddle, L., 92
Bindley, Katherine, 33–39
Bisexual, Gay, and Lesbian Alliance, 37
Black-box warning, 72
Boston University, 8
Bradshaw, Catherine, 37–38
Briggs, Winston, 32
Brown, Bill, 7

CPSIA information can be obtained
at www.ICGtesting.com
Printed in the USA
FFOW02n2059050314
4090FF